Pickles, Relishes & Chutneys

Gail Duff

Tastes, traditions, and 60 international recipes,
with notes on their origins and uses

SELECT
EDITIONS

A QUANTUM BOOK

Paperback edition published by
Selectabook Ltd.
Selectabook Distribution Centre,
Folly Road,
Roundway,
Devizes
Wiltshire SN10 2HT

This edition printed 2001

ISBN 1-86160-483-1

This book is produced by
Quantum Publishing Ltd.
6 Blundell Street
London N7 9BH

QUMPIC

Printed in Hong Kong by
Sing Cheong Printing Co. Ltd.

Pickles, Relishes & Chutneys

Contents

INTRODUCTION

Introduction

~

Preserving fruits and vegetables is a way of keeping fresh ingredients from all over the world in perfect condition in your own larder.

It is a centuries old process which can be perfected in modern kitchens.

~

INTRODUCTION

PRESERVING MAKES EXCELLENT USE OF FOODS PRODUCED IN THEIR NATURAL SEASON AND HARVESTED IN PERFECT CONDITION. BUT IT IS NOT MERELY A MATTER OF ECONOMY, CATCHING PRODUCE AT ITS PEAK, WHEN PLENTY MEANS CHEAP, FOR USE LATER IN THE YEAR. IT IS ALSO ABOUT ENJOYMENT. NATURALLY SUN-RIPENED VEGETABLES AND FRUIT, FOR EXAMPLE, CAN TASTE FAR BETTER PRESERVED THAN THE SAME BASIC FRESH INGREDIENTS FORCED TO GROW OUT OF SEASON IN WEAK LIGHT. MOREOVER, PRESERVING IS A FORM OF ALCHEMY, A MARVELLOUS TRANSFORMATION OF BASIC INGREDIENTS INTO SOMETHING ENTIRELY DIFFERENT, EXCITING AND DELICIOUS.

ABOVE: Since early times, sprigs of herbs have been put into the pickle jar for both appearance and flavour. Dill has always been one of the most popular of pickle herbs and both its feathery leaves and its seeds are used. It can be used with a range of summer vegetables but is best of all with cucumber.

Before the advent of freezers, where much of our surplus garden produce ends up, other methods of keeping harvested vegetables and fruits before they spoiled had to be devised. The drying of fruit is no doubt the oldest form of preserving fruit, but the technique of making pickles out of vegetables and fruits was already well known thousands of years ago.

The ancient Egyptians, Greeks and Romans, as well as the Celts, certainly knew all about how to alter the flavour and texture of vegetables by pickling them. During the Dark Ages the practice was carried on in the monasteries, subsequently flowering in medieval times, when it became an art learned by the mistress of every house. In the

RIGHT: Boxes full of summer's bounty, the perfect ingredients for pickles and chutneys. Here are sweet peppers of all colours to be pickled alone or with other vegetables, tomatoes for chutneys and cauliflowers to give a crunch to Piccalilli.

sixteenth and seventeenth centuries, when new ingredients were discovered in foreign lands and brought home to Europe, the cookery book, containing recipes for preserves, became a valued item in many home kitchens. Trade with India introduced chutneys and relishes to Europe, especially Britain, adding an important extra dimension to savoury preserving.

The early recipes, made in English country kitchens and preserving rooms, have changed very little over the years. Although they have been slimmed down and simplified, the basic methods and end results remain the same. In fact, the wheel seems to have gone full circle. In the seventeenth century, cooks seemed willing to pickle just about anything that was edible and ready to absorb influences from all over the world. But by the middle of the twentieth century, the English at least seemed to have limited their interest in savoury preserves to pickled beetroot, red cabbage, onions and cucumbers, many of which were commercially produced rather than prepared at home. But that is all changing now.

Today, the world is a much smaller place and many countries are more cosmopolitan. Ethnic communities have introduced their foods to alien cultures, and supermarket shelves and market stalls all over the world offer exotic fruits and vegetables to be

RIGHT: Plants of the genus Solanum, which are all related to the potato and nightshade. They include the tomato which, although at first treated with suspicion in the West, became one of the most popular ingredients for making pickles, chutneys and sauces.

1a
1b
1c
2a
7a
8a
9a
2
3
1
6
5
E.T. del. et zinc
Day & Son Lith^rs to The Queen
Solanaceæ

ABOVE: *Spicy pickled mushrooms flavoured with ginger*

experimented with. Gardening catalogues feature new baby vegetables. We now take far more interest in new foods and in the recipes of other countries than at any time since the seventeenth century.

Combine these with our old favourites and the possibilities for creating new savoury preserves are limitless.

The time is right to start pickling again and to make new chutneys and relishes. But what exactly are savoury preserves and what is the difference between them? For many people, the words "pickle", "chutney" and "relish" have become somewhat interchangeable, which is not surprising as many manufacturers' labels are equally confused. In culinary terms, however, there are clear differences between these three types of preserve which are all based on vegetable or fruits.

ABOVE: *Red wine vinegar: perfect for making pickles with red coloured and robust flavoured ingredients such as red cabbage and beetroot, or red coloured fruits such as blackberries, raspberries, cherries or plums. Buy the best quality vinegar that you can afford.*

Pickles can be made with vegetables or fruits. Vegetables are usually salted, either with dry salt or brine (a salt and water solution), before being packed into jars and covered with a spiced vinegar. Various flavourings by way of herb sprigs or spices can be put into the jars. Fruits are usually poached in a spiced vinegar syrup. Pickles are clear and the vegetables and fruits remain recognizable. Vegetable pickles are eaten while they are still crisp.

Chutneys are made from mixtures of chopped vegetables and fruits mixed with vinegar, sugar and spices and simmered for a long time until they reach the consistency of jam. They keep well over a long period during which their flavours improve and mellow.

Relishes are made in different ways all over the world. Many are rather like a cross between a pickle and a chutney, made from finely chopped and salted vegetables cooked very quickly in a vinegar mixture before being bottled. Some of these cooked relishes are thickened with flour or cornflour. Others are mixtures of puréed raw vegetables and herbs. Some raw ones contain yoghurt, others are cooked with a small amount of vinegar.

No matter where they are from or when they are used, pickles, chutneys and relishes are always an excellent extra ingredient that will complement or improve the flavour of any main dish, be it a plain roast, a curry, kebabs, tortillas or beef burgers. Their basic ingredients are very similar and most are based on fresh, occasionally dried, vegetables and fruits with the addition of salt, vinegar, oil, sugar and spices in varying proportions. There are so many different combinations and preparation methods that nearly every country in the world has its own characteristic recipes.

HOMEMADE PRESERVES

The best of these savoury preserves are homemade but there is a lot more to home preserving than simply preparing food that is good to eat. Preserving foods in our own kitchens for the use of our family and friends keeps us in touch with the traditions of past cooks and gardeners. When working through the different stages of preparation, and maybe even growing the basic ingredients in the garden, think how many other cooks, down through so many centuries, have done exactly the same thing as you are doing now.

Preserving at home also puts us in touch with the year's natural cycle, something that so many people living in cities have forgotten about. Living in centrally heated houses and flats and going to shops that sell the same frozen produce all the year round, it is easy to lose track of the passing seasons. But when you take an interest in preserving you will soon learn which fruits and vegetables are best at which times of the year, for even the imported ones have their seasons. Summer time will come to mean tomatoes and soft fruits and winter time citrus fruits and roots. This may not seem relevant today, but at one time our lives were governed by the solstices and equinoxes, by the passing of the seasons and the phases of the moon. To recognize the wheel of the year is important for every person, no matter how you do it.

RIGHT: *A selection of vinegars and spiced pickled fruits. Choose pickle jars that are both atttractive and practical. Spices for clear pickles can be tied in small pieces of muslin so they can be lifted out easily and do not spoil the appearance of the pickle.*

INTRODUCTION

Pickles, relishes and chutneys in history

~

We have inherited a great legacy of recipes and methods for making pickles and chutneys.

The first pickles were made about ten thousand years ago and methods and ingredients have been improving ever since.

~

Pickles, relishes *and* chutneys *in* history

As soon as people started to grow and farm their own food, it became necessary to find ways of preserving any surplus for the lean times, and it was probably around 10,000 years ago that acids, sugars, salt and alcohol were discovered to have preserving properties. How these worked was not understood until the end of the nineteenth century, but the fact that they did was all that mattered in the early years of civilization. Immersing food in one or a mixture of these basic ingredients, is, after drying, the most ancient method we have of preserving fruit and vegetables.

Below: Cabbages have been used for pickles since Roman times when a recipe was devised for pickling the stalks. During the Medieval period, the whole cabbage was shredded and pickled and went under the name of "pickled greens".

As soon as the fermentation process of liquids was discovered, probably accidentally, acids and alcohol became available, the acids at first being the result of unsuccessful attempts to produce alcohol. Sour wine, or the equivalent, was probably the first pickling medium. There was no sugar in those early times but honey was the main luxury sweetening ingredient and it was soon found that food swamped in honey would be exceptionally well preserved. Salt was mined in some areas and produced by panning (evaporating sea water) around the coasts.

It is known that the ancient Egyptians pickled many food ingredients between 3000 and 1000 BC. The Celts used vinegar and were probably responsible for spreading its use throughout Europe and into Britain. The Greeks made some pickles, but it was the Romans who became skilled in the process and developed recipes that formed the basis of later knowledge. Many of their ingredients were imported from all over the Roman Empire: vegetables from Europe and fruits such as lemons, peaches and apricots from Africa, the Middle East and Spain. These were used alongside home-grown herbs, roots and flowers.

Roman pickles were based on a brine of vinegar and salt mixed with olive oil, on wine must (a by-product of wine fermentation) and sometimes on pure honey. They were sealed in large, cylindrical, earthenware jars and kept for considerable periods of time, sometimes even buried in the garden to ensure an even, cool temperature.

Roman vinegar was actually sour wine, and the French origin of the English name for it, "vin aigre", means just that. Sometimes yeast, dried figs, salt and honey were added to it to make a preserving liquid. The same liquid was also watered down and used as a drink, the same one that the New Testament records as being used at Christ's crucifixion.

Two Roman writers, Apicius and Columella, have left us recipes for a wide variety of pickles, including lettuce leaves, turnips, asparagus, fennel, onions, cabbage stalks and

Right: In the late nineteenth century bought pickles and chutneys became popular, along with bottled sauces and bottled fruits. A wide selection could be bought from grocer's shops.

HARVEY'S
E.LAZENBYS
SALAD OIL
THE CELEBRATED
PICKLES
BRITISH
SAUCE
KETCHUP
LONDON
A1
CALVES FOOT JELLY
E.LAZENBY & SON
LONDON SE
PLUM
PICKLED MANGOES
WALNUTS
APRICOT
WHOLE FRUIT JAM
DAMSONS
C.W.
GRAIN VINEGAR
CHOICE MIXED
PICKLES
LONDON
HOLBROOKS
SWEET PICKLES
TART
TART
TART
TART
TART
BARNES & C
LONDON
PLUMS
CRANBERRIES
CHERRIES
PICCALILLI.
E.LASANBY.
WARRANTED
C.W.

ABOVE: Bombay, on the Malabar Coast of India, which, in the seventeenth century, belonged to the East India Company of England. From here, spices and other ingredients for pickles, such as mangoes and limes, were exported.

plums. Columella wrote in the first century AD that "vinegar and hard brine are essential for making preserves", a statement that still applies to pickles today.

When the Roman Empire collapsed in the fifth century AD, sophistications such as food preservation and pickle making were in danger of disappearing from the Western world. Fortunately, some preserves continued to be made in the monasteries where the monks grew their own food and constructed special rooms for its preparation and preservation. The rest of the population were too preoccupied with obtaining and defending land to be concerned with preserving vegetables.

CULINARY ARTS REVIVED

It was not until the eleventh century, when domestic life began to quieten down again, that the more gentle of the culinary arts began to be revived. Most large medieval houses had their own garden and some had orchards, but the range of vegetables grown was fairly small, consisting mainly of cabbages, root crops, leeks and onions, plus a selection of herbs.

Cabbages, first mentioned as "pickled greens" in a household list of 1290, appear to have been a regular ingredient for pickling. Wine, vinegar and verjuice (the sour juice of crab apples and, in later years, unripe grapes) were the main pickling liquids. Fruit was still preserved by drying or in a honey syrup.

Pickles were, as they are now, recognizable chunks of vegetable preserved in a liquid. Finely chopped mixtures of vegetables cooked to a purée with preserving ingredients were rare, although a book written by Goodman of Paris in 1393 includes a recipe for something called "compost" which consists of walnuts, turnips, carrots, pears, pumpkins, peaches, fennel and Hamburg parsley roots simmered with a large mixture of spices in quantities of wine. As it took four months to make it was probably not very popular, certainly not in the average manor house which grew only everyday vegetables.

The types of vegetables and fruits available increased during the sixteenth and seventeenth centuries as seafarers went farther afield and returned with their botanical discoveries. Mushrooms, which had been viewed with suspicion during medieval times, became one of the most popular of pickling ingredients along with walnuts, various wild plants, salad vegetables and flowers, the latter making attractive edible garnishes for salads. Great care was taken when pickling rosebuds, for example, to ensure that they kept their bright colour. Brilliant red or orange nasturtium buds were also a favourite at this time, when the decoration of food was almost an art form. Pickled vegetables were also both garnish and part of a dish. They were served with fresh vegetables, in salads and also with cooked vegetables to add a contrast in flavour. Verjuice was frequently used at this time which probably gave the pickles a much milder flavour than those of later years which were based on vinegar.

Increasing numbers of recipe books appeared during the seventeenth century and works by Gervase Markham, Robert May and John Evelyn all contain a considerable number of pickle recipes. Evelyn, writing in 1699, gives in detail recipes for diverse ingredients such as artichoke hearts, ash-keys, green beans, broom buds, elder buds, cauliflowers, cowslips, cucumbers, lemons, melons, mushrooms, radish pods, the small green fruits of the potato plant (which we would now consider poisonous), purslane, samphire and walnuts.

By the end of the seventeenth century, the increase in British trade with the East India Company had introduced many new ideas and ingredients from India, amongst them

LEFT: When the Roman Empire fell apart, the art of pickling and preserving was carried on in the monasteries. The monks were almost completely self sufficient and the sharp condiments were a welcome addition to a frugal diet.

ABOVE: A string of fresh onions, one of the earliest ingredients to be pickled and still just as important today as it ever was

mangoes, chutney and ketchups. The Hindustani word "chatni", signifying a strong, sweet relish, was very soon Westernized and has been used ever since for the thick, stewed concoctions of vinegar and vegetables.

Western cooks very soon copied the chutneys and Indian style pickles. One of the first of these new-style recipes was what we now know as Piccalilli, which first appeared in a cookery book of 1694 under the heading "To pickle lila, an Indian pickle". Because mangoes were imported into Britain already pickled, the name mango was as often used for the pickles as for the fruit itself. From John Evelyn onwards, recipe writers "made a mango" of a variety of vegetables and fruits. Evelyn's recipe, a "Mango of Cucumbers", is rather like a typically English cucumber pickle of the time with a little mustard added. Marrows, melons, peaches, plums and even apples were all in their time made into mangoes.

Throughout the eighteenth century, plain meats served with an increasing variety of pickles and chutneys replaced the old style meals of meats in sauces. More fruits were put into pickles than before, among them redcurrants, grapes and barberries. Tomatoes were used for the first time. Finally accepted as a vegetable they were made into a sour pickle with garlic, ginger and vinegar.

Wine vinegar, when it could be obtained, was the favourite liquid for pickling, along with wine itself and grape juice which had just begun to ferment but not yet become wine. The quality of the malt vinegar available commercially was very poor and many cooks in country houses made their own.

By this time, Europeans had pushed west into America, settled and established farms and gardens. Farmhouses on the east coast had special buildings for dairying, pickling and preserving. They also had big root cellars where all kinds of vegetables and fruit, such as potatoes, squash, pumpkin and apples, were stored. Down amongst the fresh produce were dried corn and beans and jars of pickles.

EIGHTEENTH-CENTURY RECIPES

In Britain, more cookery books were appearing and most included special sections on preserving and pickling. Hannah Glasse's 1774 book contained modern-sounding recipes for onions, beetroot, red cabbage and gherkins alongside the Elizabethan descendants of concoctions for asparagus, fennel, artichoke hearts, radish pods and samphire. Her main pickling liquid is wine vinegar which suggests that towards the end of the eighteenth century, pickles became more pungent and vinegary, more, in fact, as they are today. She also used large quantities of the savoury spices such as mustard seed and ginger, and horseradish, but had no recipes for chutney.

No matter what the pickling process, the colour of vegetables immersed in vinegar or brine for a certain length of time will always fade slightly. The attempt to prevent this happening led to the eighteenth-century vogue for using copper salts after it was discovered that if they were added to the vinegar, vegetables kept their green colour.

USE OF COPPER PANS

Using copper pans, which reacted with the vinegar, had the same effect and these processes were often specifically called for in cookery books. The habit was eventually called into disrepute by Elizabeth Raffald who published *The Experienced English Housekeeper* in 1782. She informed her readers that using artificial greening methods was "poison to a great degree" and advocated the strict adherence to "following strictly the direction of your receipts for any kind of pickles ... greened only by pouring your vinegar hot upon them, and it will keep a long time." She included over thirty pickle recipes in her book (cucumbers, walnuts, mushrooms, barberries, nasturtiums, elder shoots and radish pods were still popular, as were cauliflowers, beetroot and grapes), but there were still none for chutney.

THE NINETEENTH CENTURY

Moving on into the nineteenth century, *The Cook's Oracle*, published in 1822, made some excellent suggestions for making pickles, most of which are still relevant today. The instructions for spiced vinegar and the advice on the types of jars that should be used (not glazed earthenware or the lead will leach out) could, with only a few changes, be put into a modern cookery book. The actual recipes are for walnuts, gherkins, beetroot, onions, red cabbage, cauliflower and Piccalilli, a very much refined and modernized list compared with Elizabeth Raffald's recipes forty years earlier.

Later in the nineteenth century, the Victorian recipe writers Eliza Acton and Mrs Beeton gave one recipe each for "Chetney Sauce". Both recipes were said to have come from India, Mrs Beeton's specifically from Bengal, and both were based on apples and raisins although Eliza Acton's also contained tomatoes, which were becoming increasingly popular for ketchups and sauces. Neither recipe was actually a cooked chutney, though. Eliza Acton's ingredients were pounded in a mortar, mixed with spices and vinegar and bottled uncooked. Mrs Beeton's were chopped, mixed with vast quantities of salt and spices, put into a jar and covered with vinegar. After a month both "chetneys" were strained and bottled, with the vinegar being reserved separately as an addition to cooked sauces. Eliza Acton recommended using a "good genuine vinegar, French or English", or a good quality home-made one.

In the late nineteenth century, quite a variety of commercially made pickles became available, the most popular eventually being beetroot, onions, red cabbage and walnuts.

Households, however, had begun to make their own chutneys and relishes based on the original Indian recipes. In Victorian times it became the norm, when it could be afforded, to have hot roast meat on Sundays and to save enough to be eaten cold on several of the following days. Plain cold meat is not necessarily very appetizing which is why chutneys and relishes became so appealing. Making chutney – chopping the ingredients, and stewing them with vinegar and spices – was in a way a less precise process than pickling. Chutneys could also be made of mixtures of ripe ingredients. Consequently, they became increasingly popular in ordinary households, especially in country districts where there were often surpluses of vegetables throughout the summer.

Because the ingredients of a chutney very often depended upon availability at the time of making, there were few, or perhaps even no classic recipes. As a result, very few chutney recipes were ever written down. You are more likely to find favourite recipes in your grandmother's hand-written recipe book than you are in a published work of the time. Chutney making was a very personal thing. You could learn a basic method and then go your own way.

Chutneys keep well, they are easily potted and are often sold at country bazaars and on market stalls. For the past two hundred years, alongside jam, they have been the mainstay of the country cook's store cupboard. Relishes were often quickly made on the spur of the moment, again, using any ingredient that seemed appropriate and available. They kept for only a short time and then were forgotten. The old cookery books contain no relish recipes at all. The history of pickles stretches back over thousands of years while chutneys and relishes are relatively modern upstarts. All together, however, these tasty preserves have come to epitomize the country store, the thrifty use of surplus vegetables and fruits for times of shortage and the magic of creating new, wonderful flavours to enhance ordinary foods.

BELOW: In the early part of the twentieth century commercially prepared pickles became available. H. J. Heinz was one of the leading manufacturers.

INTRODUCTION

Savoury preserves from around the world

~

Every country has its own favourite savoury preserves. They can be found in shops, on market stalls and in home larders the world over. Some are traditionally eaten with bread, others with meats or rice dishes. All add that extra zest and character to whatever they are served with.

~

SAVOURY PRESERVES *from* AROUND *the* WORLD

PICKLES, CHUTNEYS AND RELISHES ARE FOUND ALL OVER THE WORLD. THEY RANGE FROM THE HUMBLE, HOME-MADE APPLE CHUTNEYS SOLD AT ENGLISH VILLAGE FETES TO THE EXOTIC SHREDDED GREENS PRESERVED IN RICE WINE THAT YOU MAY FIND GARNISHING CHINESE DISHES OF MEAT, FISH OR RICE. THERE ARE MANGO CHUTNEYS IN THE CARIBBEAN, SHARP DILL PICKLES IN EAST EUROPE, PICKLED RED ONION SLICES IN MEXICO AND QUICKLY MADE YOGHURT RELISHES IN INDIA. ALL ENHANCE OR COMPLEMENT THE MAIN DISHES THAT THEY ACCOMPANY. MANY ARE ONLY EVER MADE IN THE HOME.

BELOW: The aubergine, or egg plant, is a frequent ingredient in Middle Eastern pickles, either alone or with mixtures of peppers, cucumbers, cauliflower, baby onions and artichoke hearts.

It is not known for sure who first discovered how to preserve surplus foods in this way, but certainly it was a practice already well known in the Middle East by 3000 BC. Methods of preparation in the region have changed very little over the centuries and today many grocer's shops have large jars filled with a wide variety of colourful pickled ingredients that the proprietor or his family have prepared. Pickles are also sold from the jar by street vendors, to be eaten instantly with flat Arab bread which is dipped in the vinegar. When the jar is empty, the vinegar is sold for use at home as a basis for sauces and to liven up rice dishes.

The art of pickle making is usually learned at home and many families pride themselves on their well-stocked store-cupboard, crammed with rows of jars in which every conceivable vegetable has been immersed in pickling liquid to be served either as an accompaniment, as a snack with bread, or in place of a salad. These Middle Eastern pickles are made in a fairly standard way. The raw or slightly cooked vegetables or fruits, which are sometimes salted first, are packed into sterilized jars then covered with a cold liquid. This may be pure vinegar and salt, a mixture of vinegar and salt water in varying proportions, or a good quality oil. Great care is taken to dislodge any air bubbles from the jars which are then tightly sealed. It is a simple process but very effective and the strength and saltiness of the liquid determines the ultimate flavour and keeping qualities of the pickle. In the main, the mixture of the vinegar with water makes Middle Eastern pickles milder than those made with pure vinegar in Western countries. Herbs such as dill, garlic, hot chilli peppers and a variety of spices can all be added for extra flavour.

The most popular vegetables for Middle Eastern pickles are sweet peppers and hot peppers, aubergines, either whole or sliced, cucumbers, cauliflowers, turnips, baby onions, okra and artichoke hearts. These can be used singly or in mixtures known as *titvash*. From Iran comes *Torshi-ye hafte-bijar*, a mixture of herbs, leeks and spinach in a salted vinegar flavoured with chilli peppers, peppercorns, oregano and garlic.

A popular savoury preserve in Israel is *Zehug*, a hot relish made with fresh chilli peppers, garlic, coriander seeds and ground cumin. It originated in Yemen where it was served with beef casserole dishes on the Sabbath. Another Jewish relish, this time originating in eastern Europe, is *Chrane* (page 121), a mixture of horseradish and beetroot that is served with salt beef.

There are also many Middle Eastern fruit pickles. Lemons in oil, whole dried peaches and apricots, cherries on the stem and whole grapes are favourites. Pickled orange rinds and dates are often minced then mixed with tamarind and sumac to make a kind of uncooked chutney.

India, too, has a cuisine which values contrasting accompaniments and probably no other country in the world makes as good use of so many mixtures of spices as can be found there. It is, of course, the home of chutneys – cooked, "keeping" and fresh chutneys.

Some cooked chutneys are made in a similar way to British chutneys, in which fruit and spices are simmered together for an hour or more. For some chutneys, ingredients such as mango or pumpkin are puréed raw then cooked with the spices and vinegar for a short time only before being either bottled and stored for a long period or placed in the refrigerator for about a week only. The ingredients and preparation method determine the keeping time. Some keeping chutneys are not cooked at all. One Kashmiri chutney, for example, is made of brown sugar and vinegar mixed with large quantities of minced green ginger, garlic, mustard seed and hot peppers plus saffron and cayenne pepper. These are all mixed together, bottled and left for a month before opening, resulting in a very spicy, pungent mixture, similar in texture to a well-cooked chutney, and with long keeping qualities.

Fresh chutneys are made just before serving using a wide range of fruits, vegetables, herbs, spices and often yoghurt. In the West, they probably would be regarded as relishes. Those with a yoghurt base are sometimes called sambals or raitas. Some ingredients in fresh chutneys are puréed and some finely chopped and there is always a good flavouring of herbs and spices. Some fresh chutneys are not hot at all and are eaten to tone down the spiciness of a curry. Others have a certain amount of heat which is very often derived from fresh ingredients such as green or red chilli peppers or ginger. This gives a fresh taste to complement rich dishes of meat or vegetables.

Indian pickles are very spicy, with a certain degree of heat, and range from sweet to sour. Garlic, limes, cauliflower and aubergines are common ingredients and the preparation often involves long marination in spices and salt. For some pickles, no other ingredients are added; some are covered in oil and a few in brine.

Many pickles and keeping chutneys can be bought ready prepared in India, but the very nature of the fresh chutneys means that they are always specially prepared for every meal using ingredients that are in season and readily available. Consequently, every family has its own unique recipes which are passed down from one generation to the next.

Across India's border into China, very few pickles are made in the home although a wide range of vegetables are pickled commercially. Although the Chinese enjoy eating pickles, there are very few available recipes. Two are included in this book, a simplified version of pickled spring greens (page 57) which comes from Kweichow, and a mixture of winter vegetables in brine (page 121), sometimes called *pow tsai*, which is probably the one most often made in Chinese homes. Other pickles enjoyed by the Chinese are Szechuan hot pickle, made from cabbage or kohlrabi, and snow pickle, made from mustard greens. These two are usually bought ready made in cans. There is also a winter pickle of salted cabbage which can be bought in jars. Further east, in Japan, pickles are served with nearly every meal and, because their preparation is so simple, most are made in the home when needed.

ABOVE: Just one of the many varieties of Indian mango chutney that have been available over the years. Mango chutney has been popular in the West since the seventeenth century and the mango fruit has given its name to other imitation pickles and chutneys.

LEFT: Cabbages and long winter radishes, or mooli, being stored on the window ledge of a house in Beijing.

A popular way of ending a meal is to serve a small portion of plain rice accompanied by tiny portions of pickle. Salt or soy sauce are often used as a single pickling ingredient. Sliced cabbage or white radish can, for example, be sprinkled with either or both ingredients and left for a few days until the juices have drained from the vegetable to form a natural pickling liquid. The Relish of Red and White Radishes (page 57) is made according to this method. Crisp and light, it is ideal for a quickly made pickle. Cucumber is treated in the same way as radishes. Pickles made like this will only keep for up to a week in the refrigerator. Another typical Japanese ingredient is *kombu*, a dried seaweed which is first stewed, then chopped and mixed with vinegar, soy sauce, sugar, rice wine and sesame seeds to make a relish.

ABOVE: A pile of hot chillies in Thailand. Chillies are used in hot pickles and relishes in many parts of the world.

The simple pickling method used in Japan is also used in Korea, where the result is known as *kimchee*. Cabbage, white radish, cucumber and turnip are favourite ingredients, and garlic cloves are pickled whole in a mixture of soy sauce, rice vinegar, sugar and salt. These pickles are made at home and everyone has their own favourite ingredients.

From Indonesia and other parts of South-East Asia come sambals or sambols. These are quickly made spicy relishes that are served with rice and hot curries. They are all made at home to accompany the favourite dishes of the household. Dried, hot chilli peppers are ground with peanuts and tamarind paste, tomatoes are puréed in oil with cayenne pepper and lime juice; fresh chilli peppers are pounded with garlic, peanuts, soy sauce, lime juice, tamarind and sugar. In Ceylon a coconut sambal, made by mixing freshly grated coconut with chilli powder, browned onions, lemon juice and salt, is popular. *Seeni* sambal, also from Ceylon, is hot, rich and made from browned onions, lemon grass, curry leaves, cinnamon, tamarind, fresh chilli peppers, coconut milk and dried prawns. There are pickles, too, from the same areas, usually made by mixing the main ingredient, such as fresh pineapple or cooked aubergines, with vinegar, sugar, salt and spices. These are eaten within a week of preparation

And so to Europe, where, if one were asked what was the most pickled vegetable, the reply might well be the cucumber. There are countless recipes for pickled cucumbers, mainly for the small ones which are sometimes called gherkins or (in France) cornichons, but also for the large variety, sliced or diced. In East Europe, dill pickles, small cucumbers in vinegar with sprigs of dill and peppercorns, are the favourite. In Scandinavia they are flavoured with blackcurrant leaves and horseradish and in France with thyme, tarragon and bay. Baby cucumbers are not widely available fresh in Britain but tiny pickled gherkins bought in jars are popular with cold meats.

Cabbage is the only vegetable ingredient of German sauerkraut, a fermented pickle which takes several weeks to perfect. It is available commercially in tins and jars but many cooks still prefer to make their own. In Britain, plain red cabbage has been a popular candidate for pickling for over a hundred years. Its rich colour and crunchy texture make it an excellent accompaniment to cold meats. Also popular in Britain are pickled beetroot and pickled baby onions, made with a simple brine of spiced malt vinegar. With bread and cheese, pickled onions make a "ploughman's lunch" and they are always sold alongside fish fried in batter.

Cauliflower usually appears in mixed pickles in Europe, particularly Italy and France, and it is an essential ingredient in Piccalilli (page 99). Teamed with broccoli, it makes a light, delicate springtime pickle.

SOUTHERN EUROPE

Peppers, tomatoes and aubergines are the sun-kissed ingredients of southern Europe. They are often preserved in olive oil flavoured with garlic, tomato purée and warm spices such as paprika. Olives themselves are pickled in brine both commercially and in the home. Green olives are picked when under-ripe whereas black ones have become fully ripe on the tree. Garlic slivers, coriander seeds, and sprigs of herbs such as thyme or tarragon are all used to flavour olives.

The Europeans also specialize in making sweet pickles with seasonal fruits. In Italy, mixtures of fruits such as melon, grapes and cherries are made into a mustard pickle. Pears, quinces, plums, apricots and peaches are put into vinegar sweetened with sugar or honey. Cherries are pickled whole on the stem and

Left: Fresh limes and lemons are used to make delicious, zesty pickles and relishes in India.

even clementines and other small, sweet citrus fruits can be pickled whole, complete with their skins. Fruit pickles are generally served with cold meats.

Very special to Britain, because of her historical relationship with India, are chutneys. Not the quickly prepared, fresh chutneys, but mixtures of fruits and vegetables, nearly always including onions, simmered for a great length of time with vinegar, sugar, dried fruits and spices to the consistency of jam. Tomatoes, rhubarb, apples and marrows are other popular chutney ingredients.

There are very few relishes as such in Europe. Possibly the closest thing is Britain's mint sauce, which is served with roast lamb. It consists simply of chopped mint mixed with vinegar and a little sugar and is similar to the fresh herb chutneys of India.

From Europe, as we have seen, pickles and chutneys travelled to the United States. Cucumbers with dill rapidly became popular as did a form of Piccalilli which came to be called "Bread and Butter pickles". Cherries, green peppers, mushrooms, olives, peaches and prune plums soon found their way into the pickle jar, and it was not long before new ingredients were discovered and utilized, such as blueberries, water melon rind and sweetcorn. Chutneys also found their way to America via England directly from India through the spice trade.

American Relishes

The relish – the quickly prepared sweet-sharp mixture of vegetables which so often accompanies barbecued foods – has proved to be truly American. Corn relish, pepper relish and tomato relish have become *de rigueur* whenever burgers or steaks are grilled, whether outdoors or in. They accompany sausages, cold meats and vegetarian foods and they have travelled back to Europe in their new guise to become just as popular there.

American relishes were much influenced by the Mexican salsas, mixtures of chopped tomatoes, onions and sweet or hot peppers that are used to top a *tostada* or *enchillado*. One such Mexican relish is the "Pico de Gallo" (rooster's beak), made with tomatoes, spring onions, radishes, coriander leaves, chilli peppers and lime juice. The recipe for pickled red onion slices (page 100) is based on a Mexican one which is served with chicken and seafood.

It is not far from South America to the Caribbean, where mangoes, pawpaws and other exotic fruits are plentiful. Mangoes in particular are made into chutney, influenced by the Indian chutneys brought by the colonials of the eighteenth and nineteenth centuries. Mangoes are used when they are hard and under-ripe. They are simmered with sultanas, cashew nuts, ginger, garlic, hot red peppers, brown sugar and malt vinegar in St Kitts, and with tamarind and allspice in Jamaica. Quickly made relishes of puréed or finely chopped ripe mangoes and pawpaws mixed with lime juice and chilli peppers also come from the Caribbean.

Wherever you go in the world, you will find a pickle, a chutney or a relish to complement your meal and to tantalize your taste buds. All have been made using fresh, local produce and all show the character of the eating habits of the local people.

Below: Sweetcorn and onion, waiting to be made into corn relish, which is popular in the United States.

INTRODUCTION

The basics

~

Everything that you need to make pickles, chutneys and relishes can be found in your local shops and around your own kitchen. Choose whatever fruits and vegetables are in season and combine them with salt, sugar and vinegar, using nothing more complicated by way of equipment than a non-corrosive saucepan.

~

Ingredients

Good quality vegetables, fresh and dried fruit and herbs are the basic ingredients for all pickles, chutneys and relishes. They are combined with vinegar, salt, sugar and spices in varying proportions and in a variety of ways to achieve the desired end result.

Fresh fruit and vegetables

Although pickles and chutneys are an excellent way to make use of seasonal produce, they should never be regarded as a way of salvaging ageing or slightly below par ingredients. Fresh fruit and vegetables should always be of the best possible quality and any mouldy or diseased fruit should be compleletely discarded.

For pickling, vegetables must be young, crisp, firm and without blemish, and they need to be prepared as soon as possible after buying or harvesting so that their crispness will be maintained. Fruit for pickling should be only just ripe, so that it will remain firm and retain its shape, even if simmered in the pickling liquid.

The same rules apply to vegetables when making chutneys, although tomatoes should be ripe rather than hard and under-ripe, and fruits, such as apricots or peaches, are better if they are ripe and beginning to soften. Lower grade fruits can be used for chutneys, since they are cooked to a purée. You can use, for example, small pears or irregularly shaped apples, provided they are sound, without fear of the end result being spoiled.

Young, crisp vegetables, fruit in excellent condition and sprigs of freshly picked herbs are the essential ingredients for relishes. They are made in a variety of ways, some being slightly cooked and others being constructed from completely raw ingredients.

Dried fruits

Dried fruits are often included in chutneys to add flavour and texture as well as to replace some of the sugar. Larger dried fruits, such as apricots and dates, are usually chopped or minced and smaller ones, such as raisins and sultanas, are used whole. Buy seedless fruits of the best quality.

Whole dried fruits are also pickled and added to relishes. Raisins and sultanas can be put into vegetable pickles and in the Middle East complete dried peaches and apricots are pickled on their own.

Vinegar

As a preservative, vinegar works by penetrating and replacing the natural liquids in food, so inhibiting the growth of micro-organisms which would cause the food to spoil or "go off".

Vinegar is a sharp-tasting liquid consisting of dilute acetic acid produced as a result of the fermentation of carbohydrates into alcohol, followed by oxidation. The source of carbohydrates for the original fermentation may be fruit sugars, as used to produce wine or cider vinegars, or malted barley, as in malt vinegar.

Whichever vinegar you choose to use, must have a minimum acetic acid content of 5 per cent. All ready-bottled vinegars meet this

Opposite : A mixture of button and oyster mushrooms. These, as all vegetables should be for pickling, are in perfect condition.

Below : Dried fruits are often added to chutneys for both sweetness and flavour. There is a wide variety to choose from.

ABOVE: A 1920s advertisement for pure malt vinegar. Malt vinegar has a robust flavour and dark colour. The spiced variety is still available for quick and easy pickling.

requirement. Until recently, many country stores sold a product known as "barrelled vinegar", which was excellent for salad dressings but did not come up to strength as a pickling acid. If your local shop still stocks this, keep it for table use only.

Malt vinegar is the cheapest form of vinegar. It is dark brown in colour, has a robust flavour and is frequently used for chutneys and for all pickles where colour is not an important criterion. It is the favoured vinegar in Britain for pickling onions and eggs, its dark colour complementing the pale-coloured ingredients.

Distilling malt vinegar produces a clear, smoother-flavoured liquid that costs only marginally more than the original malt vinegar. Distilled malt vinegar enhances the colour of pickled vegetables and can help to maintain a lighter colour when making certain chutneys.

Both ordinary and distilled malt vinegar can be bought ready spiced for pickling. Although these can be great time savers, their use can mean a loss of control over the final flavour of the pickle, so care is needed.

Wine vinegars are made from fresh wines. White wine vinegar is usually slightly yellow or brown in colour, rather like a pale white wine, and has a fine, subtle flavour. It is excellent for pickling delicately flavoured ingredients such as mushrooms or asparagus. It can also be used in chutneys and relishes. Red wine vinegar is red to rose in colour, depending on the brand, and more richly flavoured than white wine vinegar. It is useful for pickling red ingredients such as red cabbage, beetroot or red onions or when making chutneys or relishes with red fruits such as plums or redcurrants.

Cider vinegar is produced from cider. It is darker in colour than white wine vinegar and has a distinctive cidery flavour. It is good for apple chutneys and relishes.

SALT

As part of the pickling process and when making some relishes, vegetables are salted – either sprinkled with salt or immersed in brine (a salt water solution). This draws water out of the vegetables which can then be replaced by vinegar. Salting also slightly toughens the vegetables, which helps to retain their crisp texture and improves the keeping qualities of a pickle.

Any non-iodized salt is suitable for pickling. Avoid iodized table salt which may darken the colours of some fruits and vegetables. Most cooking salts are non-iodized. So, too, are coarse sea salts, which are particularly suitable for this use but may be expensive. Salt sold in blocks is ideal. To separate the grains of this type of salt, rub a block on a grater or rub two blocks together.

SUGAR

Sugar acts as both a flavourer and a preservative. It is an indispensable ingredient in chutneys. Vegetables and fruits can be pickled in a sweetened vinegar syrup. And some relishes call for the addition of a little sugar.

The type of sugar used very much affects the end result. As granulated sugar forms a colourless syrup, it is often used for pickles requiring a clear visual effect. It is also useful for light-coloured chutneys. However, as long cooking of any type of sugar will produce a dark colour, for a light-coloured chutney it is wise to add the sugar towards the end of the cooking time.

Brown sugars contribute colour and flavour, and generally the very dark, soft sugars, have the richest taste. Brown sugars are often used in chutneys and relishes. Demerara sugar, which produces a light golden-coloured syrup, can be used for pickling.

ALTERNATIVE SWEETENERS

Honey, black treacle, molasses and golden syrup can all replace some of the sugar content in chutneys and relishes. They will always add colour and flavour. Honey makes a delicious pickling syrup for whole fruits such as apricots, cherries and plums. Use the same weight as you would sugar. Dried fruits can also be used as a sweetener in chutneys, replacing some of the sugar content.

SPICES

Most pickles, chutneys and relishes are flavoured with spices.

For pickles, whole spices are used to flavour the vinegar. They can be either used loose or tied up in a small piece of muslin to allow easy removal. A muslin bag is the best method for making a sweetened vinegar syrup, for instance, where the fruits are generally simmered in the syrup along with the spices. Whole spices such as dried chilli peppers, cloves or cinnamon sticks are often put into the pickle jars with the vegetables where they will continue imparting their flavour to the pickle for as long as it is kept.

In chutneys, which cook down to thick purées, spices are generally used ground. Recently bought ground spices give the best flavour; any that are older than six months should not be used.

Fresh ginger, chilli peppers and garlic are all considered as spices. Fresh ginger can be bought in the piece, peeled, thinly sliced and used in the same way as whole spices for flavouring vinegar. Chilli peppers can be cored and seeded then cut in half for flavouring vinegar or finely chopped for including in chutneys. Whole garlic cloves will flavour pickling vinegar and can be put into the jars with the vegetables. For chutneys, garlic is either crushed or finely chopped.

BELOW: A selection of fresh ingredients, waiting to be pickled

EQUIPMENT

MOST OF THE EQUIPMENT THAT YOU NEED TO MAKE PICKLES, CHUTNEYS AND RELISHES CAN BE FOUND IN ANY WELL-STOCKED KITCHEN.

CHOPPING AND MINCING

Chopping boards and good, sharp vegetable knives are essential. For chutney ingredients, which have to be chopped into very small pieces, a food processor is ideal. It will save considerable time when preparing a large quantity of ingredients. Dried fruits do not chop easily in a food processor but they can be minced, along with other ingredients such as onions, using either a hand or an electric mincer.

SALTING AND MARINATING

Salting, soaking in vinegar and marinating are normal processes in making pickles, chutneys and relishes. As the acid in salt and vinegars reacts with certain metals and can permeate absorptive materials, large bowls made of non-reactive and non-absorptive materials are essential. Dissolved metals can taint or even poison the food and although a surface that becomes permeated with vinegar or brine will not damage food in any way, the bowl may not afterwards be suitable for any other purpose. Strengthened glass, such as Pyrex, is the most suitable material. Plastic bowls may be used provided the surface is non-absorptive. Glazed earthenware is not suitable since the salt or vinegar may damage the glaze.

To cover brined or marinating ingredients use plastic wrap.

For stirring the salting or marinating ingredients choose metal spoons which will not react or corrode. Stainless steel implements are the best.

COOKING

Special preserving pans or saucepans are ideal. Although expensive to buy, they will last a lifetime if properly cared for. If possible choose ones made of stainless steel or good quality aluminium.

If ordinary saucepans are to be used, they should be made from a non-reactive material, such as stainless steel, aluminium or enamel. Those with a high quality non-stick finish are also suitable. Make sure that the coatings of enamel or non-stick pans are not chipped. Iron, brass and copper pans are not suitable. Their metals will react with vinegar, tainting the food and even, as in the case of copper, making it slightly poisonous.

Saucepans should be big enough to accommodate all the ingredients to about two–thirds full. Chutneys and vinegar syrups are very sticky and are difficult to clean off a hob should they boil over the edge of a saucepan that is too small.

Large, stainless steel or wooden spoons are ideal for stirring ingredients while cooking. If you prefer using wooden spoons, keep special ones for making vinegar-based preserves as the vinegar permeates them and may taint other foods that you subsequently prepare with them.

A large, perforated spoon, preferably stainless steel, is necessary when making pickles that have to be removed from a liquid before being put into jars. A stainless steel ladle will also be useful.

Any straining, for example of spiced vinegar, should be done through a heatproof nylon sieve.

BOTTLING

An adequate supply of jars is, of course, essential. The most convenient size of jar is one that holds 350ml/12fl oz/1 1/2 cups, generally referred to as a 500g/1lb jar since it holds by weight 500g/1lb of jam, marmalade or honey.

Purpose-made preserving jars, with either spring-clip or screw tops, are excellent for all pickles, chutneys and relishes but are not essential. If your preserves are for home use, and you make them often, it is well worth keeping a supply of these jars. If, however, you give your produce away, using these jars will prove expensive.

Strong, glass jars fitted with plastic screw

tops (such as coffee jars) or plastic-coated metal screw tops (such as peanut butter jars) are good substitutes. It is crucial not to allow any metal to come into contact with vinegar-based preserves as the metal will corrode and affect the flavour. Even when using plastic-coated tops, it is a good idea to place a disc of ceresin or waxed paper in the lid as well. Chutneys can be covered with waxed paper discs before the screw tops are put on. Press these down well, making sure that no air bubbles are trapped underneath.

Simple jam-pot covers – waxed paper discs and an outer covering of plastic film or transparent cellulose – can be used for chutneys but are only completely effective if the chutney is stored in a dry, cool, well-ventilated place for no longer than six months. After this time, the vinegar may start to evaporate and the chutney will dry out.

Some bottling jars are sealed with corks. These must be tight fitting and replaced for each bottling with new corks that have been briefly boiled. They are then covered with greaseproof paper and tied down with string.

All jars should be thoroughly cleaned and sterilized before use. To do this, wash and dry them then lay them on their sides in a very low oven (100°C/200°F/low gas) and leave them for about 15 minutes. Before embarking on the final stage of pickle or chutney making, sterilize sufficient jars ready for bottling. This will save last minute panics. Use the jars straight from the oven if the recipe calls for warm or hot jars but allow them to cool, without leaving them for too long, if the recipe calls for cold ones.

Transfer pickles, chutneys or relishes to jars using a stainless steel ladle. A stainless steel or plastic jam funnel, with a wide outlet to fit into the tops of most preserving jars, is useful.

Sticky-backed labels on which to write the type of pickle or chutney and the date made are essential. Plain ones are quite adequate for home use, but decorative ones will smarten up any produce earmarked as gifts.

ABOVE: A non-corrosive pan, sharp knives, wooden spoons, perforated spoons and ladles, jars, lids and labels: all that is needed for successful pickle and chutney making.

INTRODUCTION

Methods

~

THE TECHNIQUES OF MAKING PICKLES AND PRESERVES ARE VERY SIMPLE. TIME, AND THE CHEMICAL REACTION OF SALTS, OILS AND VINEGARS, WILL DO MOST OF THE WORK FOR YOU. STORAGE AND BOTTLING ARE THE KEYS TO A FULL STORE CUPBOARD ALL YEAR ROUND.

~

METHODS *for* MAKING PICKLES, RELISHES *and* CHUTNEYS

WITHIN THEIR CATEGORIES, CHUTNEYS AND PICKLES USUALLY INVOLVE FAIRLY STANDARD METHODS OF PREPARATION AS OUTLINED BELOW. RELISHES ARE A LITTLE MORE DIVERSE IN THEIR METHODS OF PREPARATION. THESE ARE GUIDELINES ONLY, AND INDIVIDUAL RECIPES SHOULD ALWAYS BE FOLLOWED.

VEGETABLE PICKLES

Pickles are usually made from raw vegetables that are packed into jars and covered with vinegar. The final flavour and texture of a pickle are determined by how they are treated and what other ingredients are added. The stages in making a vegetable pickle, plus a few variations and alternatives, are broadly as follows.

Initial preparation Some vegetables, such as onions or tomatoes, are peeled or skinned. Large vegetables are sliced or cut into evenly sized pieces. Small ones, such as baby onions and small cucumbers, are left whole. Others, such as beetroot, may have to be cooked before pickling.

Brining To reduce the water content of vegetables, which would otherwise dilute the pickling liquid, they are often salted, either by dry-salting or brining. Individual recipes do vary, and cooked or blanched vegetables may not need to be salted.

To dry-salt vegetables, they are first peeled and/or chopped to size. They are then layered in a bowl with salt, covered and left for 12-24 hours.

To brine vegetables, they are completely immersed in a strong salt and water solution. Many recipes give precise proportions, but a good guide is 250g/8oz/1¼ cups of salt to

RIGHT: Shredding cabbage for pickling. A sharp knife will preserve the texture and shape of any vegetable. Cut your vegetables evenly so the pickle will look attractive in the jar.

2.4litres/4pt/10 cups of water. A plate placed over the vegetables will hold them under the liquid. The bowl is then covered and the vegetables left for 12-24 hours.

After salting and brining, the vegetables are drained and usually rinsed with cold water and patted dry with kitchen paper.

Preparing vinegar Vinegar for pickling is usually flavoured with spices before being poured over the vegetables. Ideally, preparation of the vinegar starts as soon as the salting process of the vegetables begins.

The desired quantity of vinegar is poured into a non-reactive saucepan and the required spices for the recipe are added. There are usually about 3 tablespoons of spices to each 1.2litres/2pt/5 cups of vinegar. The vinegar is set over a medium heat, brought to the boil, covered and simmered for 10 minutes. The pan is then removed from the heat and the vinegar left, still covered, until it is quite cold. Cooling takes about 2 hours, depending on the surrounding temperature. The vinegar can be strained immediately it has cooled or left for as long as the vegetables are being salted, which will result in a slightly more strongly spiced flavour. The spiced vinegar is strained through a nylon sieve into a jug for easy pouring over the pickles. The spices are discarded.

To make a milder pickle, wine can be used to replace a proportion of the vinegar.

Preparing oil Oil can be used instead of vinegar for pickling. To flavour oil, whole spices, for example coriander seeds, herb sprigs or garlic cloves, are added to it. It is then covered and left in a warm place for up to 12 hours.

Bottling When the vegetables are ready they are packed into sterilized jars; warm ones if the vinegar is hot, cold if the vinegar is cold.

To flavour the pickle after it is bottled, dried chilli peppers, slices of ginger, herb sprigs, whole spices or peeled garlic cloves can be pushed into the jars with the vegetables.

The vinegar is then poured over the vegetables to completely cover them. Any air bubbles must be dispelled by shaking or tapping the jar. If the vinegar is cold, the jars are sealed immediately. If it is hot, it is allowed to cool completely before the jars are covered to prevent condensation, which would dilute the vinegar, from forming.

The jars are then labelled with the date and type of pickle.

Storing Pickles are stored in a cool, dry place. They need to be kept for at least one week before opening to allow the flavours to fully penetrate the vegetables. Most vegetable pickles maintain their crispness for up to four months.

ABOVE: Removing seeds from a honeydew melon. After this, cut the melon into wedges and cut the rind from each wedge, before evenly dicing the flesh.

FRUIT PICKLES

Fruit is usually pickled in a syrup made from vinegar and sugar or honey.

Initial preparation Small fruits, such as apricots, cherries or plums, are usually left whole. Pricking them in several places with a fork enables the vinegar syrup to penetrate more easily. The fruits are then packed into warm, sterilized jars.

Larger fruits, such as pears or peaches, are peeled. Fruits with a core (pears or quinces, for example), are quartered and the core cut away. Stoned fruits (peaches or nectarines, for example) are halved and the stone removed. The halves are either left intact or sliced.

Preparing the syrup and bottling The vinegar and sugar are stirred together into a non-reactive saucepan over a low heat until the sugar has dissolved. Whole spices to flavour the syrup are added at this point. They can be either loose or tied up in a small piece of muslin for easy removal. The syrup is boiled to release the flavours of the spices into it.

If the syrup is to cover whole fruits, it is boiled until it thickens and then is poured over the fruits. For pickling sliced fruits, the syrup is boiled briefly, the heat lowered and the prepared fruits added and simmered gently until they are cooked through but still firm. They are lifted out using a perforated spoon and packed into warm, sterilized jars. The syrup is then boiled until it thickens and is poured over the fruits.

In each case, the spices from the syrup may be either put into the jars with the fruits or removed. Additional spices, such as whole cloves, dried chilli peppers or pieces of cinnamon stick, can also be put into the jars at this stage.

The pickle is allowed to cool completely before being covered and sealed. The jars are labelled with the date and type of pickle.

Storing Fruit pickles are kept for at least one week before being opened to allow the flavours time to penetrate the fruit. Most fruit pickles will keep for up to a year if stored in a cool, dry place.

CHUTNEYS

Chutneys are usually made with a mixture of fruits and vegetables.

Initial preparation All fruits and vegetables are finely chopped or minced. After being checked over, and peeled or skinned, they can be chopped by hand or in a food processor. A mincer is useful for tougher ingredients like dates or figs.

Dried fruits may be softened by soaking in vinegar for up to 12 hours in advance, before the preparation of the fresh ingredients takes place.

Some recipes call for vegetables to be salted or brined in a similar way to pickle ingredients.

Cooking In simple chutney recipes, all the ingredients are usually put together in a saucepan or preserving pan, brought to the boil over a medium heat and gently simmered to form a thick purée with the consistency of jam. But some recipes do vary slightly.

Sugar produces a darker colour when cooked for a long time. If a pale coloured chutney is required, white sugar is added after the rest of the ingredients have cooked down.

In some recipes, all or half of the vinegar is reserved until halfway through the cooking time.

At the beginning of the cooking time, a chutney will need to be stirred only about every ten minutes. However, towards the end of the cooking time, as the chutney becomes thicker, it will need frequent stirring to prevent it from sticking to the bottom of the pan. The time that chutneys take to thicken varies from one to three hours. When they are thick, bubbling and a spoon dragged through the centre leaves an impression that lasts for a few seconds, they are ready. The chutney is removed from the heat at this point and left until it has stopped bubbling.

Bottling As soon as the chutney has stopped bubbling, it is ladled into warm, sterilized jars. Between each ladleful the chutney is pushed down and any pockets of air are dislodged. Any drips or stickiness are wiped off the jar or rim with a clean, damp cloth. The chutney is covered and sealed immediately. The jars are labelled with the type of chutney and the date.

Storing Chutneys improve and mellow with keeping so they are left for at least one month, preferably longer, before being opened. Many chutneys will keep, unopened, for up to two years and maybe more if stored in a cool, dark, dry cupboard. After this time, the level of chutney in the jar may begin to shrink as the vinegar evaporates and the contents dry out.

RELISHES

There are many different ways of making a relish. Some are a mixture of fresh ingredients, mixed together to be served immediately. Others are made in a way that is something of a cross between pickle and chutney procedures, as described below.

Initial preparation Vegetables and fruits for relishes are usually finely chopped and often lightly dry-salted or brined.

Cooking All the ingredients are put into a preserving pan or saucepan and cooked for 5-45 minutes. Some relishes are thickened by adding a mixture of flour or cornflour and vinegar to the pan. After thickening, the relish is cooked for a further 2-5 minutes.

Bottling Cooked relishes for keeping are put into warm, sterilized jars and sealed immediately. They are labelled with the date and type of relish.

Storing Bottled relishes will keep for up to six months if stored in a cool, dry place.

PEACHES:—

LEFT: Peaches make a delicious chutney, very similar to mango. They can also be sliced and put into a sweet, spiced vinegar.

RECIPES

RECIPES

Spring

~

BRING A BREATH OF FRESH SPRING AIR INTO YOUR LARDER BY MAKING SAVOURY PRESERVES WITH BOTH HOME-GROWN AND IMPORTED FRUITS.

USE YOUR IMAGINATION AND FIND VEGETABLES SUCH AS LEEKS, SPRING GREENS AND DRIED BEANS THAT YOU HAVE NEVER THOUGHT TO PRESERVE BEFORE.

~

SPRING

IN SPRING, THE AIR IS CLEAR AND FRESH, NEW LIFE BURSTS OUT OF THE GROUND AND YOU HAVE SWEPT AWAY ALL THE COBWEBS IN THE HOUSE. NOW IT IS TIME FOR SOMETHING NEW IN THE LARDER, SOME BRAND NEW SAVOURY PRESERVES FOR SPRING. BUT WHAT PRODUCE IS THERE TO CHOOSE FROM?

ABOVE: Cucumbers, once only a summer vegetable, are now grown throughout the year and are excellent in the spring. Since early times, there have probably been more recipes for pickled cucumber than for any other single vegetable.

Traditionally, springtime was still a very lean time of year, perhaps even the most precarious as the old saying makes clear: "March will tell, April will try but May will prove whether you live or die." What it meant was that with winter stores running low, there was really very little fresh produce to be had. The next season's crops were in the ground, but still only a few centimetres high. We hardly notice this today, now that food is jetted all over the world and cheats the seasons, but if you were to look at the vegetable garden in spring, what would you find?

Definitely leeks. Why else were they chosen as one of the emblems for St David's Day, 1st March (the other emblem is a daffodil)? Leeks withstand all the bad weather that winter can throw at them and actually grow in girth throughout the colder months without becoming tougher. With their green tops standing up from the ground like flags, they are the cook's promise of spring. Like onions, leeks are an excellent antidote to the common cold and many country people believed that eating leeks daily at this time of year would keep you healthy for a year. Another old saying goes:
"Eat leeks in lide [March] and ramsons [wild garlic] in May, And all the year after physicians may play."

If you grow leeks yourself, you will know just how much dirt clings to them when they are pulled up. Wash them well under running water both before trimming and cutting to length and after. There is nothing worse than a gritty leek, whether in a stew or a pickle. Even if you buy your leeks ready trimmed and washed, wash them again under cold running water after chopping to length, just in case. If you need to store leeks at all, wash them, leave them whole and put them in a polythene bag in the refrigerator for up to three days. If they are left unrefrigerated, they tend to dry up.

Unlike onions, leeks are best cooked before pickling so that they become really succulent after being steeped in the vinegar. They make an excellent accompaniment to all cold meals and are particularly good with pasta (page 55).

Broccoli is another spring garden favourite. As every plant seems to bear heads at the same time, to be able to turn them into a pickle is a great advantage. Most home gardeners grow what is known as "sprouting broccoli", which produces an abundance of small heads on side shoots. This is occasionally available in the shops but, since it is also sold with a large number of edible leaves attached, it is rather a waste to buy it simply for the heads. Instead, choose the larger-headed broccoli known as calabrese, which is also available at this time of year, and cut it into small florets. Both types of broccoli will keep in a polythene bag in the refrigerator for up to three days.

Although cauliflower is available all year, it is particularly flavoursome in spring when the hardy, overwintered varieties are ready for harvest. The crisp stems and crumbly textured florets of cauliflower have made the vegetable a favourite pickling ingredient for several centuries. Elizabeth Raffald's *Experienced English Housekeeper*, written in 1782, includes two recipes, one of which requires the salted cauliflowers to be laid out in the sun "till they are quite dry like scraps of leather" before the vinegar is poured over them. In India cauliflower stems are pickled and in the Middle East cauliflower is pickled with dill or radishes. In the West a favourite cauliflower pickle has long been Piccalilli. However, as the other vegetable ingredients are not generally

RIGHT: Spring is traditionally the time when an abundance of fruits become available, and the later months of the season are especially plentiful.

Apples
1 Kentish White Pipp.n SDE
2 Jews Pippin SDE
3 Pear Russett SDE
4 Warners Beiffin SDE
5 Kentish Pippin SDE
6 French Russetting SDE
Warners long keeping Pippin 7 SDE
8 Nonpareil SDE
9 Kentish Gold.n Pipp.n SDE
10 French gr.n Reinette SDE
11 Norfolk Beiffin SDE
12 Black Cap SDE
Cherries
13 Small May S
14 Early Duke S
Currants
15 Early Red S
16 Early White S
Pears
MAY 1732
17 May Bergamot S
18 Winter Boon from a D
19 Winter Champaign S
20 L.d Cheneys Green S
21 Old Amozell S
Strawberries
22 Wood
23 Scarlett
24 Hautboy
A Pomgranate S
B Coffee Branch
C Canada barberrie
D Blue Berried Honysuckle
E Melon thistle
F Pomplemus Orah
G Shaddock Citron
H Apple Blossom
I Pomgran.n Blossom
K Citron Lemon
L Sage Leaf Love App.le
SDEW
Design'd by P.tr Casteels.
From the Collection of Rob.t Furber Gardiner at Kensington 1732.
Engrav'd by H. Fletcher.

Above: Rhubarb is a wonderful stand-by in the spring. It grows prolifically in country gardens and is readily available in the shops. It makes a delicious chutney, especially when combined with dried fruits.

available in the spring to go with it, this is properly an autumn recipe.

Choose cauliflowers that have large, firm, very white heads. If you need to store them before turning them into a preserve, keep them in the chiller drawer at the bottom of the refrigerator for up to three days.

Spring greens, those hardy, dark green cabbages with no heart, are another successfully overwintered vegetable. It is unusual to find them in pickles in the West, but one of the few Chinese pickle recipes calls for their use (page 57).

It is unlikely that any present-day cook would run out of fresh vegetables to make into pickles, but in the eighteenth and nineteenth centuries cooks had to rely on dried vegetables, particularly beans, to see them through lean times. Kidney beans, in particular, were a popular pickle ingredient, and today chickpeas feature in Middle Eastern recipes (page 53).

Today, not only do we have efficient means of transporting vegetables but we are capable of producing them out of their once accepted season. In the northern hemisphere, cucumbers are produced in glasshouses nearly all the year round and are particularly abundant in mid- to late spring. Although the sweet, firm, outdoor-grown cucumbers are not available in spring, these are often hard to find anyway, so, for the purposes of this book, I am regarding glasshouse cucumbers as an important supplement to the supply of fresh foods in spring. Of course, you can wait until the summer to use the recipes if you wish.

There are almost more recipes for pickled cucumbers than for any other single vegetable. They come from every century and from a wide variety of countries. In East European countries they are pickled with dill, in India they are mixed with yoghurt and fresh coconut to make a refreshing sambal and in Korea they are stuffed with white radish, fresh ginger and spring onions to make a pickle called "kimchee".

The white radish, sometimes called mooli, can be made into pickles and relishes on its own or with other ingredients (page 56). In Japan, where it is known as daikon, it is made into a relish with soy sauce. Closer to home, small, round, red radishes, with a fresher, less musty taste than the white, become available in mid-spring. Use them alone or in combination with the white radish to make an interesting mix of flavours (see page 57).

Early Fruits

For spring chutney recipes, you will have to look to the available fruits. The earliest suitable fruit to arrive, often as early as February, is rhubarb. Never regarded as a luxury fruit, rhubarb is a wonderful country standby, a valuable ingredient for fruit fools, pies and crumbles when there is no other fresh fruit to be had and so prolific that most people give it away by the kilo. When cooked, it reduces down to a thick, textured purée, which makes it an ideal chutney ingredient. In fact, the edible part of the plant being the stalk, rhubarb is actually a vegetable and the slight vegetable quality about its flavour makes it blend well with onions and spices. Because of its very sharp flavour, chutneys must include plenty of dried fruits and sugar. Raisins are its natural companion, contributing sweetness and a mellow flavour to rhubarb's sharp pungency.

Fresh rhubarb should have a shiny, almost translucent quality and should be crisp and not floppy. It can be stored for up to three days in a polythene bag in the refrigerator but, like most ingredients, it is best used as soon after buying or picking as possible. Always discard the leaves as these are poisonous and trim away the end of the stalk. Otherwise, rhubarb only has to be chopped.

Early Flavours

When home-grown fruits are scarce, you can turn to more exotic ones. Melons, grown all over the world, are available all through the year, but you can really appreciate them in spring. There are many varieties, but the honeydew is the one you are most likely to find at this time of the year. It is usually pickled in a sweet-sharp solution of sweetened vinegar (page 58). Melon is best teamed with mild spices, such as cloves, cinnamon and mace, and a dark brown sugar is the best sweetener. In chutneys, melon is often treated like mango and there are various eighteenth-century recipes for "Melon, to make like mangoes", using garlic and pepper, cinnamon and mustard seed.

But why use a substitute when you can use the real thing? The most prolific of fruits, mangoes grow all over the world and are available all through the year. In the 1670s, members of the East India Company found mangoes in India where they were eaten fresh as well as being processed into chutneys and pickles. As the fruits could not withstand long sea journeys, the Company began exporting jars of pickled mangoes to Britain where they were either used as they were or turned into more elaborate chutneys with other ingredients. The name for the fruit very soon became synonymous with the pickle and many recipes were entitled "To make a Mango" and used either the original fruit or substitutes.

Mango chutney is very special. The flesh softens and stays intact and blends easily with sugar, spices and vinegar without losing its original flavour. There are mango chutneys from India, from the Caribbean (page 60) and from South Africa as well as from the country kitchens of Britain and North America. There are also what are sometimes called "fresh chutneys", mango flesh mashed and mixed with yoghurt and lime juice as an accompaniment to spicy foods (page 60).

Pawpaws are not as sweetly juicy as mangoes, but their flesh is soft and rich and, either ripe or unripe, makes a good relish (page 60).

As you can see, even an unpromising season can offer a choice of foods for preserves, from humble rhubarb to exotic mangoes. So clear out your winter larder and make way for a new supply.

BELOW: Melons of all types are available in spring. Use them like mangoes in chutney or put them into sweet, spiced vinegar.

Caribbean Mango Chutney

Very dark in colour, this is a rich, hot and fruity chutney that still maintains the fresh quality of the mango. Leave it for two weeks before opening. Once opened, it will keep for up to one month. Unopened, it will keep for up to two years.

FILLS ABOUT FIVE 500G/1LB JARS

6 under-ripe mangoes
1tbsp salt
60g • 2oz dried tamarind
250g • 8oz raisins, soaked for 12 hours
750ml • 1¼pt malt vinegar
60g • 2oz fresh ginger root, peeled and grated
2 fresh red or green chilli peppers, cored, seeded and finely chopped
2 cloves garlic, crushed
375g • 12oz dark muscovado sugar

Peel and dice the mangoes. Put them into a bowl, mix in the salt, and leave them for 2 hours. Do not drain them.Put the tamarind into a bowl, pour 6 tablespoons of boiling water over it and leave for 30 minutes. Rub it through a sieve.

Put the raisins into a preserving pan or non-reactive saucepan, pour in the vinegar and add the mangoes, the tamarind pulp, ginger, chilli peppers, garlic and sugar. Bring to the boil and simmer for about 1 hour, or until the mixture is thick. The mangoes should be tender but still in recognizable pieces.

Spoon the hot chutney into warm, sterilized jars and seal immediately.

RHUBARB *and* ORANGE CHUTNEY

This is a bitter-sweet chutney with a distinct orange flavour that goes well with cold meats. Leave it for one month before using and, once opened, eat it within one month. Unopened, it will keep for up to three years.

FILLS ABOUT FIVE 500G/1LB JARS

4 oranges, scrubbed
1.5kg • 3lb rhubarb, chopped into 2.5cm • 1in lengths
4 onions (about 500g • 1lb), finely chopped
500g • 1lb raisins
900ml • 1½pt malt vinegar
750g • 1½lb light muscovado sugar
1tsp ground mace
1tsp ground cinnamon
1tsp ground allspice

Thinly pare away the orange part of the rind and cut it into small, thin strips. Cut away and discard the white pith. Finely chop the flesh, reserving as much juice as possible and discarding as many pips as you can.

Put oranges and their rinds into a preserving pan or non-reactive saucepan. Add all the remaining ingredients. Bring them to the boil and simmer for about 2½ hours, or until the mixture is thick and dark.

Spoon the hot chutney into warm, sterilized jars and seal immediately.

INDIAN RHUBARB CHUTNEY

Keep this hot, sweet and spicy chutney for three weeks before using and, once opened, eat it within a month. Unopened, it will keep for up to two years.

FILLS ABOUT THREE 500G/1LB JARS

900ml • 1½pt malt vinegar
500g • 1lb granulated sugar
1.5kg • 3lb rhubarb, chopped into 2.5cm • 1in pieces
10 cloves garlic, crushed
1tsp cayenne pepper
2tsp ground ginger
1tbsp mustard powder
½ nutmeg, freshly grated
60g • 2oz flaked blanched almonds

Pour the vinegar into a preserving pan or non-reactive saucepan, add the sugar and set over a low heat. Stir until the sugar has dissolved. Add the rhubarb and cook gently for 20 minutes, or until it has cooked to a purée.

Add all the remaining ingredients to the saucepan. Simmer gently, stirring occasionally, for about 2 hours, or until the chutney is thick and dark.

Spoon the hot chutney into warm, sterilized jars and seal immediately.

LEMON *and* GRAPEFRUIT CHUTNEY

The rich dark brown of this unusual bitter-sweet chutney is flecked with mustard seeds and lighter pieces of citrus fruit. Leave the chutney for one month before using and, once opened, eat it within one month. Unopened, it will keep for up to two years.

FILLS ABOUT FIVE 500G/1LB JARS

8 lemons
2 grapefruit
8 onions (about 1kg • 2lb), finely chopped
2tbsp salt
250g • 8oz sultanas
750g • 1½lb Demerara sugar
2tbsp mustard seeds
900ml • 1½pt white wine vinegar

Scrub the lemons and grapefruit and finely chop them, flesh and skin together, removing as many pips as possible. Layer the citrus fruit and onions in a bowl with the salt. Cover and leave for 24 hours.

Put the citrus fruit and onions directly into a preserving pan or non-reactive saucepan, without draining them. Add all the remaining ingredients and mix well. Bring them slowly to the boil and simmer for 2 hours, or until the chutney is thick and dark.

Spoon the hot chutney into warm, sterilized jars and seal immediately.

Pickled Cucumbers

Slightly salty and flavoured with herbs, these crisp cucumber slices should be left for two weeks before using. Once opened, they must be eaten within a week. Unopened, they will keep for up to three months.

FILLS ABOUT FIVE 500G/1LB JARS

4 large or 8 small cucumbers
125g • 4oz salt, plus 1tbsp
6tbsp chopped fresh dill or fennel
2tsp dill or fennel seeds
2tsp coriander seeds
2tsp black peppercorns
900ml • 1½pt white wine vinegar

Wipe then thinly slice the cucumbers, without peeling them. In a large bowl, dissolve the 125g/4oz of salt in 1.2 litres/2pt of water then put in the cucumber and leave for 2 hours.

Pour the vinegar into a non-reactive saucepan with the remaining 1 tablespoon of salt. Bring to the boil then remove from the heat and allow to cool.

Drain the cucumber slices in a colander and rinse them well under cold water. Layer them with the chopped fresh dill or fennel and the seeds and peppercorns in cold, sterilized jars. Pour in the vinegar and seal immediately.

Cauliflower *and* Broccoli Pickle

Florets of cauliflower and broccoli make crunchy pickles, in this case, hot and spicy. Leave the pickle for at least three days before using. Once opened, it should be eaten within one week. Unopened, it will keep for up to three months.

FILLS ABOUT THREE 500G/1LB JARS

900ml • 1½pt white wine vinegar
2tsp coriander seeds
2tsp cumin seeds
2 dried red chilli peppers
1 piece fresh ginger root, bruised
1 small firm cauliflower
2 large firm heads broccoli, or calabrese (about 750g • 1½lb)

Pour the vinegar into a non-reactive saucepan, add the coriander and cumin seeds, the chilli peppers and the ginger root and bring to the boil. Cover and simmer for 10 minutes. Remove the pan from the heat. Allow the vinegar to cool completely then strain it.

Cut the cauliflower and broccoli into small florets. Bring a pan of water to the boil, put in the cauliflower and broccoli and cook them for 1 minute. Drain them in a colander and run cold water through them. Allow them to cool.

Pack the cauliflower and broccoli into cold, sterilized jars and pour the vinegar over them. Seal immediately.

HOT SPICED CHICKPEAS

An interesting addition to the range of spring preserves in the larder, this hot, tomato-flavoured pickle is Middle Eastern in origin and ridiculously easy to make. Serve it as a garnish to salad dishes. Do not use for at least one week. Once opened, the chickpeas should be eaten within a few days. Unopened, they will keep for up to two months.

FILLS ABOUT TWO 500G/1LB JARS

2 x 425g • 15oz cans chickpeas
2tbsp tomato purée
2 cloves garlic, crushed
2tsp ground paprika
½tsp cayenne pepper
150ml • ¼pt olive oil
450ml • ¾pt white wine vinegar

Drain the chickpeas and pack them into cold, sterilized jars.

Put the tomato purée, crushed garlic, paprika and cayenne pepper into a bowl and gradually work in the olive oil, 1 tablespoon at a time, to make a smooth paste.

Gradually beat in the vinegar. You can use a hand mixer or, alternatively, put all the ingredients together in a food processor and work until smooth.

Pour the mixture over the chickpeas and seal immediately.

A PICKLE *of* LEEKS *and* PINE KERNELS

A winter vegetable that overlaps into spring, leeks make a succulent pickle mixed with pine kernels and flavoured with sweet spices. Leave the pickle for at least one week before using and, once opened, eat within two weeks. Unopened, the pickle will keep for up to four months.

FILLS ABOUT FOUR AND A HALF 500G/1LB JARS

900ml • 1½pt white wine vinegar
1 cinnamon stick
2tsp allspice berries
2 blades mace
2 chips nutmeg (the small slivers left over when a whole nut has been freshly grated)
8 large leeks (about 2kg • 4lb total weight)
125g/4oz pine kernels

Pour the vinegar into a non-reactive saucepan and add the cinnamon, allspice berries, mace and nutmeg. Bring them to the boil, cover and simmer for 10 minutes. Remove the saucepan from the heat. Allow the vinegar to cool completely and strain it.

Wash the leeks well, cut them into 2.5cm/1in lengths and wash them again. Bring a pan of water to the boil. Put in the leeks and cook them for about 7 minutes, or until they are just tender. Drain and allow them to cool.

Pack the leeks into cold, sterilized jars, sprinkling pine kernels in between. Pour the cold vinegar over them and seal immediately.

ABOVE: *Mooli and Cucumber Raita and Relish of Red and White Radishes*

MOOLI *and* CUCUMBER RAITA

In India, long white radishes are known as mooli. Mixed with cucumber and a gently spiced yoghurt they make a refreshing relish to accompany curry. The relish should be served as soon as possible after it is made as it will not keep.

MAKES ABOUT 400G/14OZ

1 small white radish or mooli (about 200g • 7oz)
½ large cucumber
6tbsp natural yoghurt
1tsp ground turmeric
1tsp ground coriander
¼tsp cayenne pepper
30g • 1oz sultanas, finely chopped

Finely grate the white radish and finely chop the cucumber. Mix them together in a bowl.

Stir in the yoghurt, turmeric, coriander, pepper and sultanas. Mix well and serve.

RELISH *of* RED *and* WHITE RADISHES

Radishes grow fast and abundantly in spring and this crisp, light relish, good with curries and rice dishes, makes excellent use of them. The relish is ready to eat as soon as it has been prepared but it can be safely kept in the refrigerator, covered, for up to one week.

MAKES ABOUT 300G/10 OZ

1 small white radish or mooli (about 200g • 7oz)
20 round red radishes
4 spring onions, chopped
2 cloves garlic, crushed
1tsp salt
1tsp granulated sugar
¼tsp cayenne pepper

Cut the white radish into 1cm/½in cubes and thinly slice the red radishes. Put all the radishes into a bowl and mix in the onion, garlic, salt, sugar and cayenne pepper.

Transfer the mixture to a jar and cover with a piece of thin cotton material secured with an elastic band. Leave for 3 days at room temperature, occasionally pushing the radishes beneath the liquid that will collect.

Replace the cotton cover with a lid and place the relish in the refrigerator for 1 hour.

CHINESE PICKLED GREENS

Very light, salty and hot, and with sweetness from the sherry, this pickle keeps the fresh flavour of the greens. Used sparingly, it is an excellent accompaniment for Chinese rice dishes. Although the preparation spans several days, the method itself is very easy. Leave the pickle for six weeks before using. Once opened, use it within two weeks. Unopened, it will keep for up to six months.

FILLS ABOUT TWO 500G/1LB JARS

3 heads open green cabbage hearts or spring greens (about 1kg • 2lb total weight)
6 cloves garlic
3tbsp salt
2tbsp dry sherry
1tbsp chilli powder
2tsp caster sugar
450ml • ¾pt medium sherry

Preheat the oven to 150°C/300°F/gas mark 2.

Finely shred the greens and crush the garlic. Put them together into a casserole and cover. Place in the preheated oven and cook for 30 minutes. Remove the casserole and leave the vegetables to stand, covered, for 2 hours.

Sprinkle the vegetables with 1 tablespoon of the salt and the dry sherry. Cover again and leave to stand for 3 days at room temperature.

Mix in the remaining salt, the chilli powder and sugar, then pack the pickle into cold, sterilized jars. Pour in the medium sherry and seal immediately.

MELON *and* MUSTARD PICKLE

Sweet melon cubes in a savoury mustard sauce make this bright yellow pickle rather intriguing. Keep it for at least two days before using and, once opened, eat it within two weeks. Unopened, it will keep for up to six months.

FILLS ABOUT FIVE 500G/1LB JARS

2 large honeydew melons (1.5-1.6kg • 3-3½lb each)
750g • 1½lb granulated sugar
2tbsp mustard powder
1tbsp ground turmeric
2tsp ground ginger
2tbsp cornflour
300ml • ½pt white wine vinegar

Cut the melon flesh from the rind and remove the seeds. Cut the flesh into 1.5cm/½in dice.

Put 250ml/8fl oz of water into a non-reactive saucepan with 500g/1lb of the sugar. Set over a low heat and stir until the sugar has dissolved. Put in the melon pieces and simmer gently in the syrup for 10 minutes, or until they begin to soften and look translucent. Remove the pan from the heat and drain the melon, reserving the syrup.

In another bowl, mix together the mustard powder, turmeric, ginger, cornflour and half the vinegar. Put the remaining vinegar into a non-reactive saucepan and bring it to just below boiling point. Stir in the mustard mixture and continue stirring until it boils and thickens. Remove the pan from the heat and stir in 300ml/½pt of the reserved syrup. Stir in the melon pieces.

Put the hot pickle into warm, sterilized jars and seal immediately.

SWEET *and* SOUR CUCUMBER RELISH

With a slight Chinese flavour, this light-textured sweet and sour relish is good with poultry or lamb as well as vegetarian rice dishes. The relish is best served immediately after it is prepared but it will keep for up to three days in a covered container in the refrigerator.

MAKES ABOUT 400G/14OZ

1 large cucumber
1 onion
2tsp cornflour
1tsp ground ginger
150ml • ¼pt white wine vinegar
1tbsp soy sauce
2tbsp sunflower oil
1tbsp honey

Wipe and very finely chop the cucumber, leaving the skin on. Very finely chop the onion.

Put the cornflour into a small bowl with the ginger. Gradually mix in the vinegar and soy sauce.

Heat the oil in a saucepan on a low heat. Put in the chopped onion and cook it for about 1½ minutes, or until it begins to look transparent. Stir in the cucumber, the cornflour mixture and the honey. Raise the heat to medium and bring the mixture to the boil, stirring constantly. Stir on the heat until the cucumber is in a thickened sauce, about 1 minute.

Remove the saucepan from the heat and turn the relish into a bowl to cool completely. Serve the relish as soon as it has cooled.

Mango Relish

Nothing can beat a good mango and this hot, spicy relish keeps all the fresh fruit flavour. Mangoes are often sold hard, but can be ripened at home, wrapped in newspaper and kept in a warm place such as the kitchen. Serve the relish on the day that it is made or store it in a covered container in the refrigerator for up to three days.

MAKES ABOUT 250G/8 OZ

3tbsp sunflower oil
2 green chilli peppers, cored, seeded and finely chopped
2 cloves garlic, crushed
1tsp ground cumin
1tsp ground coriander
1 ripe mango, peeled and finely chopped
4tbsp white wine vinegar

Heat the oil in a frying pan over a low heat. Put in the chilli peppers and garlic and stir on the heat for 1 minute. Add the cumin and coriander and continue stirring for a further 1 minute.

Add the mango and the vinegar to the pan and mix. Let the vinegar come to the boil and immediately remove the pan from the heat.

Put the relish into a bowl and allow to cool completely.

Pawpaw Relish

Light and fruity, this is a relish that goes well with cold meats and fish such as poached trout, salmon, or smoked mackerel. It is best eaten on the day that it is made.

MAKES ABOUT 250G/8OZ

1 ripe pawpaw
1 small onion
1 green chilli pepper, or more to taste
½ lime, juice only
2tbsp chopped fresh coriander

Halve and peel the pawpaw. Scoop out and discard the tiny black seeds from the centre. Finely chop the flesh. Finely chop the onion. Core, seed and finely chop the chilli pepper.

Put the chopped pawpaw, onion and chilli together in a bowl, pour in the lime juice and mix well.

Thirty minutes before serving, place in the refrigerator to chill.

Right: *Pawpaw Relish*

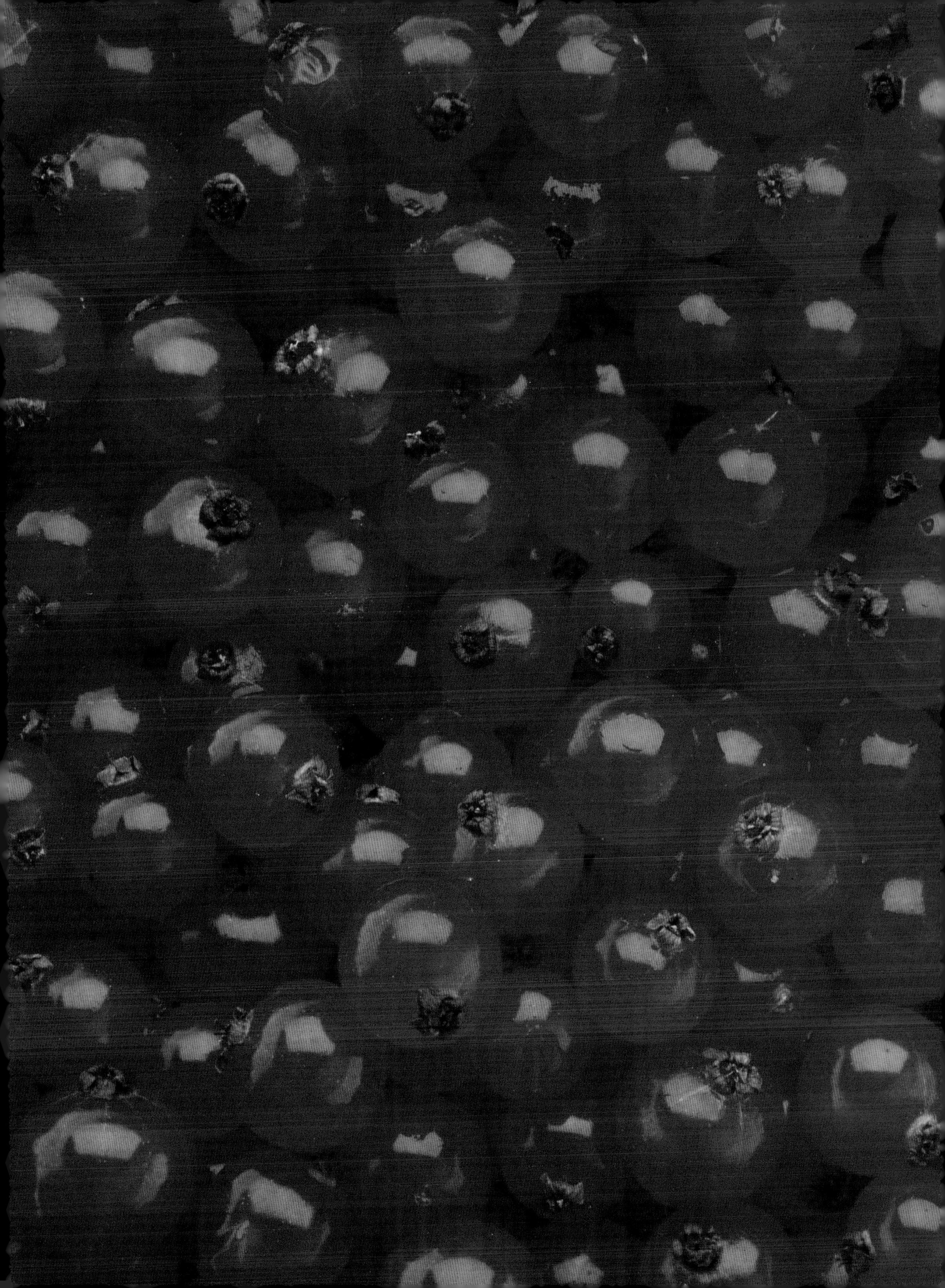

RECIPES

Summer

~

SUMMER PRESERVES REFLECT THE SEASON'S WARMTH AND ABUNDANCE. FOR MANY MONTHS TO COME, YOUR JARS OF SUMMER FRUITS AND VEGETABLES WILL ADD COLOUR TO YOUR LARDER AND THE FLAVOUR OF THOSE SPECIAL MONTHS OF THE YEAR TO YOUR TABLE.

~

SUMMER

AS SUMMERTIME PROGRESSES AN INCREASING SUCCESSION OF DIFFERENT FRUITS AND VEGETABLES RIPEN. EACH FOLLOWS THE OTHER, PROVIDING A TIMETABLE FOR SUMMERTIME PRESERVING.

All this bounty comes in a wide variety of rich colour. There are jewel-like redcurrants and blackcurrants, soft, deep red raspberries, black cherries, the blushing yellows of peaches and apricots and the deep pink of watermelon flesh. There are bright green herbs for relishes and for adding in sprigs to pickle jars; green walnuts and the soft shades of asparagus and broad beans. Later on there are red tomatoes, green, red and yellow sweet peppers, deep purple aubergines and rich red plums. By the end of the season, your larder can be lined with jars packed with brightly coloured pickles, chutneys and relishes; these jars will evoke the heady atmosphere of summer for many months to come.

Despite their wonderful appearance, soft fruits rarely figure prominently in recipes for pickles, chutneys or relishes. Although raspberries can be used to flavour vinegar, vinegar does not seem to be used to flavour raspberries. However, raspberries can make a delicate pickle that is excellent with cold meats. If you would like to try this unusual accompaniment, follow the recipe given for blackberries (page 102), but reduce the final simmering time to five minutes instead of ten. For pickling, choose the plumpest raspberries you can find and make sure that they are not over-ripe; in fact, slightly under-ripe is preferable. Always use them on the day of purchase.

Blackcurrants and redcurrants are not used for chutneys because their delicate flesh boils down to nothing during the long cooking time required, leaving only the pips. They do, however, make excellent, fresh-tasting relishes. The short cooking time required softens the flesh without destroying its structure and their sharpness provides much of the necessary acidity without your having to add large quantities of vinegar. As with raspberries, always use blackcurrants and redcurrants on the day of purchase and make sure that the fruit is sound. Remove the stalks before cooking; this slightly tedious job is well worth the effort.

Cherries are an early summer delicacy. Their season is short and they all ripen together. In medieval times, before much preserving was done, "cherries on the rise" (on the twig) were hawked through the streets. In those days fresh fruit was scarce for much of the year so everyone ate as many cherries as they could so as not to waste them — sometimes with disastrous consequences! By the sixteenth century, cooks had learned how to preserve cherries, with the result that consumption of the fresh fruits could be more moderate and the residue could be enjoyed throughout the rest of the year.

BELOW: Cherries, apricots and raspberries can all be pickled whole in spiced vinegar. Choose them when they are firm and fresh.

RIGHT: A basketful of summer fruits painted in 1732. Plums, peaches, nectarines, cherries, and green walnuts all make delightful savoury preserves.

JULY
1732
N°
S.D.E.W.
1 Roman E
2 Transpar.t } Apricock E
Cherries.
3 Italian SDEW
4 Morelo SDEN
Figgs.
5 W.t Marseilles SDEE
6 Blew Marseilles SDEW
Nectarins.
7 Nutmeg E
8 Early hastive E
Peaches.
9 Bella Chevereuse S
10 Early Ann S
11 Albermarle E
12 Montabon E
13 Rambouillet W
14 Rosanna W
15 French minion DES
16 Muske violet EE
17 Early George S
18 Early kenington E
Plumbs.
19 Violet DEW
20 Damaske de Tours DEW
21 Mirabella SDEW
22 Orleans SDEN
23 Semiano DES
24 Precoce de Tours DEE
25 Green gage SDEW
26 Morroco SDEN
27 Without stone SDE
28 Diapre noir DES
29 Amber SDE
30 W.t Imperiall DE
31 Drap d'ore DES
32 Matchless DEW
33 Black damaske SDEW
Pears.
34 W.t Robert SDE
35 Jargonell DE
36 Muscat de Ete DE
37 Lepargne DE
38 Orange muscat SDE
39 Green sugar SDE
40 Musk blanquit SDE
41 Champaigne Currant N
42 July grape DES
A Bird Cherry S
B Makaleb Cherry S
C Harts tongue Cereus
D Indian Figg
Design'd by P.tr Casteels.
From the Collection of Rob.t Furber Gardiner at Kensington 1732.
Engrav'd by H. Fletcher.

RIGHT: Young asparagus tips can be pickled in a mild vinegar, either alone or with mixtures of other summer vegetables.

Cherries are usually pickled whole, without stoning, and often with about 2.5 cm/1in of their stalk intact for easy handling when they are served. Pack them into clean jars and cover them with a vinegar spiced with mace, coriander and black peppercorns. Alternatively, the vinegar can be sweetened and the cherries simmered in it for two minutes before bottling. Choose large, plump cherries for pickling and process them on the day of purchase.

Apricots arrived in the Western world at the time of the Crusades and by the sixteenth century many country houses had apricot trees growing against south facing walls. By the end of the seventeenth century, apricot trees were already being grown next to farmhouses and settlements in America.

Like cherries, apricots had to be used up quickly, so they were often used for preserves, both sweet and savoury. They were sometimes pickled whole in a sweet, spiced vinegar. In the eighteenth and nineteenth centuries, when chutneys and relishes became popular, apricots were found to be an ideal ingredient. Their flesh actually tastes better cooked than raw and they cook down to a soft, creamy textured purée that blends well with other ingredients. For pickling, choose apricots that are only just ripe, pale yellow with a soft pink blush. For chutneys, choose them riper and deeper coloured if possible. Apricots will keep in a cool larder for up to two days or in the refrigerator for up to four days but, like most fruits, they are best used on the day of purchase.

The name for apricot comes from the Portuguese "albricoque" which in turn derived via Arabic from Greek and Latin roots meaning "early ripening" because it ripened before the peach. Peaches, like apricots, were grown by sunny farmhouse walls and later in the large greenhouses that it became the fashion for every well-to-do country house to have. Peaches were taken to South America by the Spanish in the sixteenth century and a hundred years later vast orchards were established in California. Also like apricots, peaches have long been a favourite pickle ingredient. A popular eighteenth-century recipe has them pickled in mustard-thickened vinegar, rather like a sweet Piccalilli. In chutneys, peaches behave very similarly to mangoes in that their flesh softens but remains in pieces or slices. Any recipe for mango chutney can be used for peaches. For pickling, choose peaches that are just ripe and for chutneys they should be ripe and juicy but not soft. The fruit will keep in a cool larder for up to two days.

Watermelon, with its crisp pink flesh resembling sweetened ice crystals, is harvested throughout the summer. In the seventeenth century watermelons were taken by African slaves to America where the rind soon became a common pickle ingredient. The flesh is too delicate for any sort of cooking or preserving process, but thrifty housewives soon discovered how not to waste all that rind. Soaked overnight in brine and simmered in a spiced, sweetened vinegar, it was transformed into a tasty pickle that would last through the winter.

At summer's end, come the plums. Many varieties are grown all over the world. Some are dessert varieties and others are better for cooking or preserving. Plums make a rich chutney — fruity flavoured but slightly sharp (page 68) — and, with similar ingredients, they make a good, quickly prepared relish. Pickled plums have been popular in Europe since the seventeenth century. They are usually put into a sweetened vinegar, spiced with cloves, cinnamon and allspice.

SUMMER SAVOURIES

Along with the summer fruits are the summer vegetables. Most prized of all for savoury preserving of all kinds must be the tomato (in reality a fruit, of course). Small ripe tomatoes can be pickled whole in either sweetened or unsweetened vinegar (page 76). Tomato relishes are made all over the world: the Mexican salsas, for example, often with chilli peppers and sweet peppers; the American tomato relish served so often with burgers and other fast food; the hot relishes of the Middle

East and the Indian tomato sambal.

When the tomato first arrived in the West from South America in the sixteenth century, it was looked on with great suspicion. Some regarded it as poisonous, some as an aphrodisiac (hence its old name "love apple"). It was not really until the early nineteenth century, when chutneys became popular, that the tomato came into its own, and if anyone has only ever made one type of chutney in their life, it is more than likely that it was based on tomatoes. As with cherries and apricots, if you grow your own tomatoes you tend either to have none at all or to have more than you can eat at any one time. Not surprisingly, at the end of the summer, the smell of tomato chutney wafts out from many a country kitchen. For the other ingredients, most people use whatever they have in their larder at the time. Some use sultanas, others raisins; some white sugar, some brown and some may even put in molasses. There are as many tomato chutney recipes as there are cooks that have made it.

Sweet peppers and green chilli peppers are grown all over the world all through the year, but they are still essentially summer vegetables, their crisp textures and fresh flavours making ideal hot weather food. It took a long time for peppers to be accepted in the West, particularly in Britain yet, on looking at old recipe books, you will find that even Mrs Beeton had a recipe for "Pickled Capsicums", in which the peppers are halved and seeded, brined and then put into a vinegar spiced with ground mace and nutmeg. Besides pickling, sweet peppers are used for quickly prepared relishes. From Bulgaria there is "Liutenitsa" which uses 500g/1lb each of sweet green peppers and chilli peppers; from Tunisia a cucumber and pepper relish; and from Mexico, the various "salsas" in which peppers are mixed with tomatoes (page 72). Because peppers do not cook down to a purée they are never the main ingredient of a chutney. They are, however, often a complementary ingredient, such as in a tomato chutney, where they add both flavour and texture.

Although aubergines, or egg plants, like peppers, are now available all year, they are essentially a summer vegetable. They came originally from the Middle East, where they are pickled in mixtures of spiced vinegar and oil. In South-East Asia they are made into relishes and pickles and in Japan they are served as a relish with a mustard and miso (fermented soya bean) dressing.

The green vegetables of summer – asparagus, green beans and broad beans – can all be put into light pickles, alone or together.

Unusual Delicacies

There are also some more unusual summer pickles. Pickled walnuts, picked when the nuts are green and with an undeveloped shell, soft enough to be pricked right through with a pin, have been popular in Britain since the sixteenth century (page 83). Unfortunately you cannot buy green walnuts; you have to be lucky enough to have access to a tree. Ash trees, however, grow wild, and you can pickle ash-keys (the seed pods) when they are immature, green and crisp in the middle of summer. Another summer pickle, perhaps the bonus of gardeners who leave their radishes in the ground so that they flower and seed, is pickled radish pods. The colours, textures and flavours of summer pickles are virtually boundless.

LEFT: Walnuts for pickling should be picked when they are green and tender and when a needle can be easily pushed through the outer covering, shell and kernel.

PLUM CHUTNEY

Plums make a sweet, fruity, dark purple chutney and adding apples gives a good, thick texture. Leave it for one month before using. Once opened, it should be eaten within 2 months. Unopened, it will keep for up to two years.

FILLS SIX TO SEVEN 500G/1LB JARS

1kg • 2lb plums, halved, stoned and chopped
2 large cooking apples (about 500g • 1lb), peeled, cored and chopped
4 onions (about 500g • 1lb), chopped
500g • 1lb raisins
250g • 8oz Demerara sugar
1 tsp ground ginger
1 tsp ground allspice
½tsp ground cloves
½tsp ground nutmeg
¼tsp cayenne pepper
600ml • 1pt malt vinegar

Put all the ingredients into a preserving pan or non-reactive saucepan and bring them gently to the boil. Simmer for about 1 hour, or until the chutney is thick, stirring occasionally.

Spoon the hot chutney into warm, sterilized jars and seal immediately.

PEACH CHUTNEY

This fruity, dark coloured chutney is interestingly spiced with curry flavours. Leave it for two weeks before using but once opened, eat it within one month. Unopened, it will keep for up to one year.

FILLS ABOUT TWO 500G/1LB JARS

8 peaches, ripe but firm
2tsp salt
2tsp ground ginger
2tsp ground cumin
2tsp ground coriander
125g • 4oz Demerara sugar
300ml • ½pt distilled malt vinegar

Halve, stone and finely chop the peaches. Put them into a preserving pan or non-reactive saucepan with the rest of the ingredients. Bring gently to the boil and simmer, stirring occasionally for about 2 hours. The pieces of peach should stay intact but they will soften and become coated in a small amount of dark syrup.

Spoon the hot chutney into warm, sterilized jars and seal immediately.

RIGHT: Plum Chutney and Peach Chutney

NATURAL RED TOMATO CHUTNEY

Take advantage of the summer's tomato glut to make a chutney with a natural savoury flavour and a bright orange-red colour. It makes a wholesome replacement for bought ketchup. Keep it for two months before using and, once opened, eat it within one month. Unopened, it will keep for up to two years.

FILLS ABOUT FOUR 500G/1LB JARS

2kg • 4lb ripe tomatoes
3 onions (about 385g • 12oz), finely chopped
450ml • ¾pt distilled malt vinegar
250g • 8oz granulated sugar
1tbsp salt
1tsp ground cloves
1tsp ground nutmeg
1tsp ground allspice

Put the tomatoes into a large bowl. Pour boiling water over them and leave them for 1 minute. Drain them and skin them, then finely chop them.

Put the skinned tomatoes and onions into a preserving pan or non-reactive saucepan with 150ml/¼pt of the vinegar. Bring gently to the boil and simmer for about 30 minutes, or until the onions are soft.

Add all the remaining ingredients and simmer for a further 1½ hours, or until the chutney is thick.

Spoon the hot chutney into warm sterilized jars and seal immediately.

AUBERGINES PICKLED *in* OIL

Slices of salted lemon lighten the flavour of this rich pickle. Try to buy unwaxed lemons; alternatively scrub them well. Leave the pickle for at least three weeks before using. Once opened, it should be eaten within two weeks. Unopened, it will keep for up to four months.

FILLS ABOUT TWO 500G/1LB JARS

2 lemons
1½ tbsp salt
3 large aubergines (about 375g • 12oz each)
2tsp ground paprika
200ml • 7fl oz olive oil, approximately

Wipe and thinly slice the lemons. Put them into a bowl and sprinkle them with 1 tablespoon of the salt. Leave them for 1 hour then drain them.

Cut the aubergines into 1cm/½in thick slices. If their circumference is large, cut them in half crossways. Bring a pan of water to the boil, put in the aubergines and simmer them for 7 minutes, or until they are soft but firm. Drain them and pat them dry with kitchen paper.

Put the cooked aubergine slices into a bowl. Mix together the remaining salt and the paprika and add to the aubergines. Toss to make sure that the slices are evenly coated.

Pack the aubergines into cold, sterilized jars, putting in two lemon slices between each layer. Pour in the olive oil to cover them completely. Seal immediately.

Tomato *and* Green Pepper Relish

Good with burgers, sausages and all barbecue food, this rich tomato relish can be served immediately or it can be kept in a covered container in the refrigerator for up to two weeks.

MAKES ABOUT 1.25KG/2½LB

8 tomatoes
4tbsp olive oil
1 onion, finely chopped
1 clove garlic, finely chopped
1 green sweet pepper, cored, seeded and diced
1 small green chilli pepper, cored, seeded and diced, optional
2tbsp dark muscovado sugar
4tbsp malt vinegar

Put the tomatoes into a large bowl. Pour boiling water over them and leave them for 1 minute. Drain and skin them.

Heat the oil in a saucepan over a low heat. Put in the onion and garlic and cook them for 2 minutes. Stir in the sweet and chilli peppers and cook for a further 2 minutes, stirring occasionally, until they begin to soften.

Turn the heat up to medium and put in the tomatoes. Stir to heat through. Stir in the sugar. When it has melted, add the vinegar and bring it to the boil. Remove the pan from the heat and allow the relish to cool completely.

Peach Relish

Good with curries, rice dishes or plain meats, this fruity relish can also be made with one teaspoon of hot curry powder in place of the paprika and cayenne. It can be eaten on the day that it is made, or it can be kept in a covered container in the refrigerator for up to five days.

MAKES ABOUT 250G/8OZ

2 ripe peaches
4tbsp olive or sunflower oil
1 small onion, finely chopped
1tsp ground paprika
¼tsp cayenne pepper
4tbsp white wine vinegar

Put the peaches into a bowl and pour hot water over them. Leave them for 1-2 minutes depending on ripeness. If the skin will peel off easily after 1 minute, they are ready to peel. Drain them and then skin and finely chop them.

Heat the oil in a saucepan over a low heat. Put in the onion and cook for about 3 minutes until soft. Increase the heat to high and stir in the peaches. Sprinkle in the paprika and cayenne then pour in the vinegar. Let the vinegar boil then remove the pan from the heat. Allow the relish to cool completely.

REDCURRANT RELISH

Good with poultry, game and lamb, this fruity, sharp-sweet relish can be served immediately or it can be kept in the refrigerator in a covered container for up to one week.

MAKES ABOUT 150G/5OZ

4 tbsp olive or sunflower oil
1 small onion, finely chopped
4 juniper berries
4 allspice berries
2tsp honey
250g • 8oz redcurrants, stringed
4tbsp red wine vinegar

Heat the oil in a saucepan over a low heat. Put in the onion and cook it for about 3 minutes to soften it.

Crush the juniper and allspice berries together using a mortar and pestle. Mix the crushed spices with the honey, then add the redcurrants and onion. Increase the heat to high. Pour in the vinegar, stir, and bring to the boil. Remove the pan from the heat and allow the relish to cool.

GREEN PEPPERS *layered with* AUBERGINE RELISH *in* SPICED OIL

This is a rich pickle of contrasting flavours. Leave it for two weeks before using and once opened, eat it within one week. Unopened, the pickle will keep for up to one year.

FILLS ABOUT SIX 500G/1LB JARS

8 small green sweet peppers
2 aubergines
2 onions
6tbsp salt
600ml • 1pt olive oil
1tbsp coriander seeds
1tbsp cumin seeds
150ml • ¼pt white wine vinegar

Very finely chop the aubergines and thinly slice the onions. Put each separately in a bowl. Sprinkle the aubergines with 4 tablespoons of the salt and the onions with 2 tablespoons. Cover them and leave for 12 hours. At the same time, put the olive oil into a bottle or bowl and add the coriander and cumin seeds. Leave it for 12 hours.

Rinse and drain the aubergines. Bring a saucepan of water to the boil. Put in the aubergines and simmer them for 5 minutes or until they are soft but still intact. Drain and allow them to cool. Rinse the onions with cold water and drain them well. Mix together the aubergines and onions.

Core and seed the peppers and cut them into thin, lengthways strips.

Layer the peppers with the aubergine and onion mixture in cold, sterilized jars. Strain the oil and pour it into the jars, taking care that all the spaces in the jars become filled. Seal immediately.

HOT SPICED RED TOMATO CHUTNEY

Darker than the Natural Red Tomato Chutney (p70), this chutney has a hot, spiced flavour. Keep it for two months before using and, once opened, eat it within one month. Unopened, the chutney will keep for up to two years.

FILLS ABOUT TWO 500G/1LB JARS

2kg • 4lb ripe tomatoes
4 onions (about 500g • 1lb), finely chopped
2 cloves garlic, crushed
450ml • ¾pt distilled malt vinegar
250g • 8oz granulated sugar
1tbsp ground paprika
1tsp cayenne pepper
2tsp mustard seeds

Put the tomatoes into a large bowl. Pour boiling water over them and leave them for 1 minute. Drain them and skin them, then finely chop them.

Put the skinned tomatoes into a preserving pan or non-reactive saucepan with the onions, garlic and 150ml/¼pt of the vinegar. Bring to the boil and simmer for about 30 minutes or until the onions are soft.

Add the remaining ingredients and simmer for a further 1½ hours, or until the chutney is thick.

Spoon the hot chutney into warm sterilized jars and seal immediately.

SWEET PICKLED TOMATOES

The slices of tomato in this sweet, mildly spiced pickle are tender and have a natural, red colour. Leave the pickle for one week before using. Once opened, eat it within two weeks. Unopened, it will keep for up to four months.

FILLS ABOUT TWO 500G/1LB JARS

2kg • 4lb tomatoes, ripe but not soft
4tbsp salt
600ml • 1pt white wine vinegar
625g • 1¼lb demerara sugar
2 cloves garlic
2 blades mace
1 cinnamon stick
2tsp allspice berries

Wipe the tomatoes and cut them crossways into 0.5cm/¼in thick slices. Put them into a bowl, layering them with the salt. Cover them and leave them for 24 hours. Drain them.

Put the vinegar into a non-reactive saucepan with the sugar. Peel the garlic cloves and tie them in a piece of muslin with the mace, cinnamon stick and allspice berries. Put the muslin bag into the pan. Bring the vinegar to the boil over a medium heat, stirring for the sugar to dissolve.

Put in the tomatoes, lower the heat, and bring the vinegar slowly back to the boil. Simmer for 1 minute more.

Carefully lift out the tomatoes using a fish slice and pack them into warm, sterilized jars.

Bring the vinegar back to the boil and boil for about 15 minutes, or until it is thick. Allow it to cool slightly then pour it over the tomatoes. Allow the pickle to cool before sealing.

A Mixed Pickle *of* Summer Vegetables

FILLS ABOUT SEVEN 500G/1LB JARS

1 small cauliflower, cut into small florets
250g • 8oz French beans, topped, tailed and cut into 2.5cm • 1in lengths
8 small carrots, thinly sliced
2 yellow sweet peppers, cored and seeded and cut into 2.5cm • 1in strips
2 red sweet peppers, cored and seeded and cut into 2.5cm • 1in strips
4 red or green chilli peppers, cored and seeded and very thinly sliced
16 spring onions, cut into 2.5cm • 1in lengths
6-7 garlic cloves (one per jar), peeled
6-7 fresh dill sprigs (one per jar) or fennel sprigs
900ml • 1½pt white wine vinegar
90g • 3oz salt

Leave this light, crunchy, colourful pickle for at least six weeks before using. Once opened, it will keep for up to two weeks. Unopened, it will keep for up to four months.

In a large bowl, mix the cauliflower, French beans, carrots, sweet peppers, chilli peppers and spring onions together. Then pack them into cold, sterilized jars, distributing the smaller quantities such as the chilli peppers and spring onions equally. Put 1 garlic clove and 1 dill sprig into each jar.

Pour the vinegar into a non-reactive saucepan, add the salt and 900ml/1½pt of water. Set the saucepan over a high heat and bring the contents to the boil. Remove from the heat and allow to cool slightly. Pour the vinegar solution over the vegetables and seal immediately.

CORIANDER *and* MINT RELISH

With a beautiful, bright green colour and a fresh, hot flavour, this relish is good with all Indian curries. It is best eaten the day it is made, but it may be kept in the refrigerator in a covered container for up to three days.

MAKES ABOUT 400G/14OZ

60g • 2oz chopped fresh coriander
1 green chilli pepper, seeded and chopped
2tbsp freshly squeezed lemon juice
30g • 1oz fresh mint
2tsp grated fresh ginger root (or bottled ginger purée)
½tsp salt
6tbsp natural yoghurt

Put 1 tablespoon of the coriander into a food processor with the chilli pepper, lemon juice and 2 tablespoons of water and blend to a purée. Add half the remaining coriander and blend again. Add the mint, ginger and salt and blend to a smooth, green purée. Add the remaining coriander and blend again.

Put the yoghurt into a bowl and mix in the contents of the blender. Place in the refrigerator and chill for 30 minutes before serving.

CREOLE RELISH

With a fresh, clean, hot tomato flavour, this relish will keep in a covered container in the refrigerator for up to one week.

MAKES ABOUT 875G/1¾LB

6 tomatoes (about 500g • 1lb)
½ lime, juice only
1tsp salt
¼tsp cayenne pepper
1 onion, finely chopped
1 stick celery, finely chopped
4 pimento-stuffed olives, finely chopped

Put the tomatoes into a large bowl. Pour boiling water over them and leave them for 1 minute. Drain and skin them.

Put the skinned tomatoes into a food processor with the lime juice, salt and cayenne pepper and work them to a purée.

Put the onion, celery and olives into a bowl. Mix in the tomato purée. Cover, place in the refrigerator and chill for 30 minutes before serving.

Sweet Spiced Apricots

Whole apricots are used in this mildly spiced honey pickle. Serve it with cold meats and pâtés. Leave the pickle for one month before using. Once opened, it will keep for one month. Unopened, it will keep for up to nine months.

FILLS ABOUT SIX 500G/1LB JARS

1.5kg • 3lb apricots
24 cloves or 4 per jar
2.5cm • 1in piece cinnamon stick per jar (approximately 6)
900ml • 1½pt white wine vinegar
500g • 1lb honey

Prick the apricots all over with a fork and pack them into cold, sterilized jars. Put 4 cloves and a piece of cinnamon stick into each jar.

Put the white wine vinegar and honey into a non-reactive saucepan and stir them over a low heat until the honey has dissolved. Raise the heat to medium and bring the syrup to the boil. Boil it for 5 minutes or until it is beginning to thicken.

Remove the saucepan from the heat and allow the syrup to cool slightly, then pour it over the apricots. Leave the pickle until it is cold before sealing.

ITALCAPS

PICKLED WALNUTS

If you have access to the fruit of a walnut tree, you are indeed fortunate and will be able to make this mild, onion-flavoured pickle of soft walnuts. The walnuts have to be green, that is when you can easily push a pin through both the outer coating and the young shell. The process of salting the walnuts is spread over nine days, but is well worth the effort. Leave the walnuts for at least two weeks before using and, once opened, eat them within one month. Unopened, they will keep for up to two years.

FILLS ABOUT TWO 500G/1LB JARS

1.5kg • 3lb green walnuts with skins
1.5kg • 3lb 6oz salt
4 shallots
6 cloves garlic or 2 per jar
2tbsp preserved grated horseradish
1.75litres • 3pt malt vinegar

Wash the walnuts. Put them into a large bowl and cover them with boiling water. Leave them until the water has cooled completely. Dissolve 180g/6oz of the salt in 1.75litres/3pt of cold water.

Wearing polythene or rubber gloves so as not to stain your hands, take the walnuts out of the water one by one and scrape off the thin outer skins then drop each immediately into the brine. Leave them to soak for 24 hours.

Drain the walnuts. Put them into a bowl and pour boiling water over them. Leave them to cool. Make fresh brine with the same quantities as before and soak the walnuts in this for a further 24 hours. Repeat the process seven more times.

After the last soaking in brine, drain the walnuts, put them into a bowl and cover them with cold water. Leave them for 10 minutes and drain them again.

Thinly slice the shallots. Peel the garlic cloves and leave them whole.

Pack the walnuts into cold, sterilized jars, putting in pieces of shallot, two garlic cloves per jar and a little of the horseradish.

Pour the vinegar into a non-reactive saucepan and bring it to the boil. Allow it to cool to lukewarm then pour it over the walnuts. Seal immediately.

RECIPES

Autumn

In Autumn, with so much fresh produce available pickling and preservation become almost a necessity.

Be like the squirrel and line your store-cupboard with rows of glowing pickles and chutneys to take the end of summer into the beginning of winter.

AUTUMN

AUTUMN IS THE SEASON OF PLENTY, WHEN MORE FRUITS AND VEGETABLES ARE READY FOR HARVESTING THAN AT ANY OTHER TIME OF THE YEAR. THE ABUNDANT PRODUCE OF SUMMER'S END – JUICY TOMATOES, CRISP SWEET PEPPERS, FRESH GREEN BEANS AND FAT MARROWS – OVERLAPS WITH THOSE SPECIAL INGREDIENTS THAT MAKE THEIR BRIEF APPEARANCE DURING THOSE FEW MONTHS LEADING UP TO THE END OF THE YEAR – SQUAT PUMPKINS, GOLDEN QUINCES, NUTS, WILD MUSHROOMS AND, OF COURSE, GREEN TOMATOES THAT WILL RUN OUT OF SUNSHINE BEFORE THEY ARE ABLE TO RIPEN. THERE ARE ALSO THE ROBUST VEGETABLES THAT WILL SEE US RIGHT THROUGH THE COLD OF WINTER – THE MANY KINDS OF ONIONS, THE CABBAGES, THE FIRST CELERY AND MAIN-CROP CARROTS.

ABOVE: Apples are at their best in the autumn months. Use them to make thick, sweet-sharp chutneys.

It is a rich time, indeed, when the activities of pickling and preserving, always a pleasure, almost become a necessity. It would be a pity to waste home-grown produce or neglect the store bargains going cheap, so you are tempted to stock up with rows of glowing pickles and chutneys to enjoy during the bleak season ahead. Blackberries suddenly are everywhere – wild ones in the hedgerows and their cultivated brothers in the shops. Even the most timid of wild food gatherers must have been blackberry picking at some time in their life and experienced the double satisfaction of not only having made an excellent preserve, but of actually having gone out to gather the ingredients instead of finding them on a supermarket shelf. Although wild blackberries are not as uniformly fat and succulent as cultivated ones, they often have a finer flavour, and seasoned blackberry pickers usually have their favourite patch where they know the fruits grow large and sweet.

While there is plenty of advice on how to make blackberry jam, there are few written recipes for making savoury preserves. The pips render blackberries unsuitable for chutney, but they do make an excellent pickle that goes well with red meats and game (page 102). Blackberries should be used as soon as possible after picking or buying. It is advisable to rinse both types of fruit in cold water before use, and drain them well.

Another fruit that you can find both wild and cultivated is the damson, like a small, dark purple plum with a soft blue bloom on its skin. In the United States, dark red Sierra plums, the beach plum and the Chickasaw plum can be used instead. All of these fruit are small, with a bitter flavour when raw. Although there are no recipes for pickled damsons, they do make good relishes (page 90). Damsons will keep for up to four days in the refrigerator but are best used on the day of purchase or harvest. When preparing damsons for making a chutney, it is best to stone them first. This is slightly time consuming but well worth the effort.

Apples and pears are now available all year round, but, in the Northern Hemisphere at least, they are all harvested in the autumn. This is when you can buy them straight from the tree instead of from the cold store. Modern methods of storage are wonderful but there is still nothing like freshly picked fruit. It has all of its crispness, its flavour and its juiciness. Using fruit at this time of year ensures the best possible quality preserves.

The old way of preserving apples for the winter was to cut them across into rings and hang these on sticks stored in the attic or barn

RIGHT: Apples and pears from the eighteenth century. The favourite way of using pears at the time was to pickle them whole in a sweet, spiced vinegar.

A
B
C
Apples S.D.E.W.
1 Windsor Pearm.n SDE
2 Red Cour pendue SDE
3 White Calvil SDE
4 Wheelers Rufset SDE
5 Broad'ee SDE
6 Red Calvil SDE
7 Golden Pearmain SDE
8 Silver Pippin SDE
Grapes
9 Malmise S
10 Restling or Renish W
11 White Muscatell S
12 Warners l.e Spanish S
13 Blue Goswell EE
14 White Madera S
Pears
15 Grasan DEE
NOVEMBER
1732
16 Oxford Gold.n Grasan SDEW
17 Lashafserie DEW
18 Rouslet D La Reine DEE
19 Amadott DE
20 Virgo luce DEW
21 Monsieur John SDE
22 Bezy D Hyver DE
23 Spanish boon SDE
24 Ambrett DEE
25 Angelica DEW
26 Golden Bell SDE
27 Mashes gr.n butter DEE
28 Rough S.t Germain DE
29 S.t Andrew DEW
A The Maple leav'd Service S
B Great Bullefs S
C Yellow Haugh SD
Design'd by P.tr Casteels.
From the Collection of Rob.t Furber Gardiner at Kensington 1732.
Engrav'd by Jam.s Smith.

RIGHT: Nearly every gardener who grows tomatoes has green ones left over in the autumn. They can be pickled whole in a sweetened vinegar or used to make a pungent flavoured chutney.

to dry. In the nineteenth century, when chutneys became popular, apples, especially the cooking varieties with their ability to cook down to a fluffy purée, were recognized as the ideal ingredient. There are even recipes of the time called "mango chutney" but which contain no mangoes at all, just apples, dried fruit and spices. Although apples are not usually the main ingredient for a pickle, Mrs Beeton included in her original book of 1861, a recipe for "An Excellent Pickle", which consisted of diced cooking apples, cucumber and onions in a pickling liquid of soy sauce, sherry and vinegar.

Because of their firmer texture, pears are often made into a pickle, usually with a liquid made from sugar and vinegar (page 96). They can be diced, sliced, quartered or even, if small, left whole, and put into jars with cloves or red chilli peppers to add to the flavour and appearance. Ripe pears also make a good chutney.

The quince is available only in the autumn and usually only direct from small producers or from your own garden. Golden yellow and shaped like a small, waisted pear, this unusual fruit has a rich, honeyed, pungent flavour. It can be pickled, like a pear, becoming a deep pinky-gold colour when cooked in the liquid, or it can be chopped and added to apple chutneys, using fewer quinces than apples because of their stronger flavour. Quinces keep well in a cool, dry larder for about two weeks.

All kinds of nuts arrive in the shops in the autumn and the shelled kernels can be included whole in sweet pickles or ground and mixed with herbs, onions or garlic and yoghurt to make sambals and relishes. The kernels of recently picked nuts have a fresh, crisp and milky texture.

GREEN TOMATOES

The greenhouse and the sunny garden produce dozens of green tomatoes in the autumn. In countries with a temperate climate, most gardeners are left with many late-formed tomatoes which will never ripen outside due to lack of strong sunshine. Most end up in pickles and chutneys. Once skinned, green tomatoes cook down to a fluffy purée similar to apple purée and so are an ideal ingredient for chutneys and relishes (see pages 93 and 99). Small tomatoes can be pickled whole, in a sweet-sharp syrup of sugar and vinegar, spiced with a few cloves.

Marrows are another vegetable that grow all through the summer. But as they are so prolific it is rare for them to all end up as a savoury vegetable. Their sheer abundance, as well as a natural aptitude, has made them a popular preserving ingredient since the eighteenth century. It was discovered very early on that they made an excellent substitute for mangoes in a chutney and there are many recipes for what is called "Marrow Mangoes" (page 95). They have an excellent light texture, but plenty of spices are needed to turn them into a robustly flavoured chutney.

A relative of the marrow is the pumpkin. Taken to the United States by the Pilgrim Fathers it quickly became a favourite vegetable there. Its creamy-textured golden flesh cooks down to a smooth purée, making it an ideal ingredient in chutneys (page 91). It can also be cubed to make a glowing gold pickle.

Sweetcorn is often used fresh for relishes. Frozen and tinned sweetcorn is available all the year, but the firm texture of kernels which have been freshly cut from the cob is far superior.

Onions and shallots are harvested at the beginning of autumn. Onions are indispensable to most chutneys, adding the essential savouriness to sweet fruits and sugar. Pickled baby onions have been popular in Britain since the eighteenth century and, together with cheese, have made up many a farm worker's lunch. They can be salted in plain spiced vinegar or in a sweetened vinegar. Shallots can be treated in the same way. Sliced large onions make an unusual onion pickle, whether you use white fleshed or red fleshed varieties (page 95).

Garlic, also harvested in early autumn, is often added in small quantities to chutneys and pickles as part of the flavouring, but it can also be the main ingredient, especially in relishes. For instance, mixed with some green chilli peppers and coriander and pounded together in a little olive oil or water, it makes a biting, refreshing relish which regularly accompanies dishes in India and is also known in Jewish cooking as *Zehug*.

Plentiful Mushrooms

Mushrooms are artificially grown and sold all year round now, but many nostalgic country dwellers still think of them as autumn treats. There is nothing quite like walking through orchards on a crisp, dewy morning and filling a basket with mushrooms. Few people are lucky enough to be able to do this today, so buy the commercially grown ones and allow their scent to conjure up for you pictures of misty lanes on autumn mornings as you pickle them (page 93). There are dozens of old recipes for pickling mushrooms, the reason being that they were once so abundant in autumn that it seemed as if you only had to walk past a spot and they would grew up behind your back.

International Flavours

Many autumn vegetables can be put into mixed pickles: the crisp, mustard-coated combinations known as Piccalilli and based on an old Indian recipe (page 99); the green tomato and chilli pepper pickles of Mexico; or the carrot, green bean, pepper, cucumber or cauliflower pickles of the Middle East. Mixed pickles are an excellent way of using up small surpluses of a variety of vegetables. With this type of recipe you can often substitute one for another or vary the quantities according to what you have available.

An unusual pickle from Britain worth mentioning is pickled nasturtium seeds. The British once had a liking for capers, small, pickled buds with a pungent flavour, which were mostly imported. In the sixteenth century it was discovered that the seeds of nasturtium flowers, if pickled as soon as the flowers had wilted, would make an excellent substitute. Nasturtium seeds pickled in vinegar have a pungent flavour similar to that of capers but with a slight peppery overtone. They are an easy pickle to make. Methods vary, but basically, after being dry-salted or soaked in brine, they are rinsed, drained and dried then packed into a jar, together with a few herbs such as tarragon or dill and peppercorns if desired, and covered with a white wine vinegar; some people spice the vinegar first. As there is virtually no preparation and the quantities involved are small, nasturtium seeds are a good introduction to autumn pickling.

Below Wild mushrooms, as well as the cultivated, can be pickled, but it is important to know whether they are safe to eat or not.

Quince *and* Apple Chutney

The apples in this sweet, golden brown chutney cook down to a thick purée but the small, lighter coloured pieces of quince remain more firm. Store the chutney for one month before using. Unopened, it will keep for up to two years.

FILLS SIX TO SEVEN 500G/1LB JARS

8 quinces (about 500g • 1lb)
4 large cooking apples (about 1kg • 2lb)
12 onions (about 1.5kg • 3lb)
500g • 1lb sultanas
2tsp ground mace
2tsp ground cloves
600ml • 1pt cider vinegar
750g • 1½lb Demerara sugar

Peel, core and finely chop the quinces and apples. Finely chop the onions.

Put the chopped quinces, apples and onions into a preserving pan or non-reactive saucepan, with the sultanas, mace, cloves and vinegar. Bring them gently to the boil and simmer for 20 minutes, or until the apples are soft.

Stir in the sugar and continue to simmer, stirring occasionally, for 1½ hours, or until the mixture is soft and thick.

Spoon the chutney into warm, sterilized jars while it is still hot and seal immediately.

Damson *and* Date Chutney

Rich, thick and dark, this sweet chutney makes excellent use of tough-skinned damsons, small blue-black plums which are too tart to be eaten raw. The riper the damsons are, the easier they are to stone; run a sharp knife all round each one, pull the two halves apart and then ease out the stone. Keep the chutney for one month before using. Unopened, it will keep for up to two years.

FILLS ABOUT THREE 500G/1LB JARS

1.5kg • 3lb damsons, stoned
500g • 1lb stoned dried dates, finely chopped
180g • 6oz dark muscovado sugar
1tbsp mustard seeds
1tsp ground allspice
450ml • ¾pt red wine vinegar

Put all the ingredients into a preserving pan or non-reactive saucepan and bring gently to the boil. Turn down the heat and simmer gently, uncovered, for about 1¼ hours, or until the mixture becomes very thick.

Spoon the chutney into warm, sterilized jars while it is still hot and seal immediately.

PUMPKIN CHUTNEY

Golden brown with a creamy texture, this is a good savoury chutney. Leave it for at least two weeks before using. Unopened, it will keep for up to one year.

FILLS SIX TO SEVEN 500G/1LB JARS

1.5kg • 3lb pumpkin
8 ripe tomatoes (about 500g • 1lb)
4 onions (about 500g • 1lb)
2 large cooking apples (about 500g • 1lb)
250g • 8oz sultanas
500g • 1lb light muscovado sugar
2 tsp salt
1tsp freshly ground black pepper
2tsp ground ginger
1tsp ground allspice
750ml • 1¼pt distilled malt vinegar

Cut the rind and seeds from the pumpkin and discard then finely chop the flesh. Bring a saucepan of water to the boil, add the pumpkin and simmer for 10 minutes. Drain well and mash to a purée.

Skin the tomatoes. Cut a cross in the skin at the base of each and place them in a bowl. Cover them with boiling water, leave for 10-30 seconds, then plunge them into cold water. Peel off the skin.

Cut each skinned tomato in half. Scoop out the seeds, rub them through a sieve and reserve the juice and flesh. Finely chop the flesh.

Finely chop the onions. Peel, core and finely chop the apples.

Put the chopped onions, apples, tomato flesh and juice into a preserving pan or non-reactive saucepan, add all the remaining ingredients and bring gently to the boil. Reduce the heat and simmer gently for 2 hours, or until the chutney is thick.

Spoon the chutney into warm, sterilized jars while it is still hot and seal immediately.

GREEN TOMATO CHUTNEY

Those who grow their own tomatoes are always on the look-out for a new recipe to use up unripened fruit before the frosts arrive. This is a light, fresh-tasting chutney with a good green colour. Leave it for at least two weeks before using. Unopened, it will keep for up to one year.

FILLS ABOUT FOUR 500G/1LB JARS

1.5kg • 3lb green tomatoes
2 green sweet peppers
3 onions (about 375g • 12oz)
3 cooking apples (about 750g • 1½lb)
250g • 8oz granulated sugar
1 lemon, grated rind and juice
1tbsp salt
1tsp freshly ground black pepper
1tsp ground mace
1tsp ground ginger

Put the tomatoes into a saucepan and cover them with water. Bring gently to the boil and simmer them for 15 minutes. Using a slotted spoon, remove and skin one tomato at a time, keeping the unskinned ones immersed. Cut the tomatoes in half, scoop out the seeds then rub them through a sieve and reserve the flesh and juice. Finely chop the flesh.

Core, seed and finely chop the sweet peppers. Finely chop the onion. Peel, core and finely chop the apples.

Put the tomato flesh and juice with the chopped peppers, onion and apple into a preserving pan or non-reactive saucepan and add all the remaining ingredients. Bring them gently to the boil and simmer for up to 2 hours, or until the mixture is thick.

Spoon the chutney into warm, sterilized jars while it is still hot and seal immediately.

LEFT: Mushrooms Pickled in White Wine

MUSHROOMS PICKLED *in* WHITE WINE

Preserved in a light wine and vinegar pickle, these mildly spiced mushrooms retain all of their succulence. Leave the pickle for at least one week before using. It will keep for up to two months, but once a jar has been opened, the pickle should be eaten within a few days.

FILLS ABOUT SIX 500G/1LB JARS

900ml • 1½pt white wine vinegar
2 dried red chilli peppers
2 blades mace
1 small piece dried root ginger, bruised
1.5kg • 3lb button mushrooms
2tbsp salt
350ml • 12fl oz dry white wine, plus extra for topping up as necessary
sprigs of thyme, one for each jar, optional

First, prepare the spiced vinegar. Pour the vinegar into a non-reactive saucepan and add the chilli peppers, mace and ginger. Bring to the boil, lower the heat and simmer, covered, for 10 minutes. Allow the vinegar to cool completely and then strain it.

Spread the mushrooms out on a flat dish, sprinkle them with the salt and leave them for 30 minutes. Drain the mushrooms but do not rinse them.

Put the drained mushrooms into a wide-based saucepan and set them over a low heat. Cook them for about 3 minutes, turning them occasionally, until their juices begin to run. Increase the heat and cook, stirring, for 5 minutes, until they are cooked through and have produced their own juices.

Pour in the spiced vinegar and simmer the mushrooms in it for 10 minutes. Remove the saucepan from the heat. Allow the mushrooms to cool then put them and the vinegar into a plastic container. Cover and leave for 24 hours.

Strain the mushrooms, reserving the vinegar, and pack them into warm, sterilized jars. Measure the vinegar (there should be about 350ml/12fl oz) and mix it with an equal quantity of dry white wine. Pour the liquid over the mushrooms. If there is insufficient liquid to cover them distribute what there is evenly between the jars and then top up with more white wine.

Push one thyme sprig into each jar, if you like. Seal the jars.

Sweet Spiced Onion Slices

Gently spiced with cloves, this is a sweet onion pickle. Small button mushrooms can be pickled in the same way: peel them and salt them whole, then proceed with the recipe as for sliced onions. Leave the pickle for one week before using. Unopened, it will keep for up to four months but once opened, it should be eaten within one week.

FILLS ABOUT FIVE 500G/1LB JARS

12 onions (about 1.5kg • 3lb)
2tbsp salt
600ml • 1pt white wine vinegar
250g • 8oz granulated sugar
1tbsp cloves
12 dried red chilli peppers

Slice the onions very thinly into rings. Layer them in a bowl with the salt, cover and leave for 12 hours. Rinse the onions with cold water and drain them well.

Put the vinegar, sugar, cloves and chilli peppers into a non-reactive saucepan and stir them over a low heat until the sugar has melted. Bring to the boil and simmer for 5 minutes.

Pack the onions into warm, sterilized jars. Pour the hot vinegar over them, ensuring the cloves and chillies are evenly distributed among the jars. Seal immediately.

Marrow Chutney

Tasting like mangoes after a long simmering, as so many early marrow chutneys recipes were designed to do, this hot, spicy and sweet mid-brown chutney is good with curries. Leave for at least one week before using. Unopened, the chutney will keep for up to one year.

FILLS ABOUT FIVE 500G/1LB JARS

1 large or 2 small marrows (about 2kg • 4lb)
6 onions (about 750g • 1½lb)
1kg • 2lb Demerara sugar
2 lemons, grated rind and juice
2tbsp ground coriander
1tsp ground cumin
1tsp cayenne pepper
2tsp salt
1 litre • 1¾pt white wine vinegar

Peel the marrow. Cut it into quarters and remove and discard the pips and pith. Cut the flesh into 0.5x2.5cm/¼x1in pieces. Thinly slice the onions.

Put the chopped marrow and sliced onions into a preserving pan or non-reactive saucepan together with all the remaining ingredients and bring gently to the boil. Lower the heat and simmer, stirring occasionally, for about 3 hours, until the pieces of marrow are very tender and the juices reduced and thickened. The chutney will not look as thick as one that cooks to a purée, for example apple chutney, but it will thicken as it cools.

Spoon the chutney into warm, sterilized jars while it is still hot and seal immediately.

Pickled Pears

Tender, mildly spiced slices of pear in a sharp-sweet pickle are an excellent way to make use of cheap and plentiful fruit in the autumn. Keep the pickle for one week before using. Unopened, it will keep for up to six months. Once opened, it must be eaten within one week.

FILLS ABOUT FOUR 500G/1LB JARS

1 stick cinnamon, broken
6 cloves
1 small piece dried ginger root, bruised
600ml • 1pt white wine vinegar
750g • 1½lb granulated sugar
6 small pears (about 2kg • 4lb)
dried chilli peppers, one for each jar

Tie the cinnamon, cloves and ginger root in a small piece of muslin.

Put the spice bag into a non-reactive saucepan with the vinegar and sugar. Set the saucepan over a low heat and stir until the sugar has dissolved. Bring the syrup to the boil and remove the saucepan from the heat.

Bring a saucepan of water to the boil. Meanwhile, peel and quarter the pears and cut out their cores. Put the pears into the boiling water, cook them for 5 minutes then drain them.

Bring the syrup to the boil again and add the pears. Turn the heat down and simmer for about 15 minutes, until they are tender but still firm and they appear translucent.

Using a slotted spoon, lift the pears out of the syrup and pack them into warm, sterilized jars. Put one dried chilli pepper into each jar.

Remove the spice bag from the syrup and boil the syrup again for about 5 minutes, or until it is thick. Pour the hot syrup over the pears. Seal immediately.

PICCALILLI

Almost any combination of crunchy vegetables can be used to make this perennial mustard pickle, but the selection below works very well. Leave the pickle for one week before using. Unopened, it will keep for up to three months. Once opened, it should be eaten within two weeks.

FILLS ABOUT SIX 500G/1LB JARS

1 large cucumber
1 small marrow or 6 courgettes (about 500g • 1lb)
1 large cauliflower (about 1kg • 2lb)
4 onions (about 500g • 1lb)
2tbsp salt
900ml • 1½pt distilled malt vinegar
1tbsp mustard seeds
1tsp black peppercorns
4 dried red chilli peppers
125g • 4oz Demerara sugar
2tsp ground ginger
1tbsp ground turmeric
1tbsp mustard powder
2tsp plain flour

Wipe but do not peel the cucumber and cut it into 1cm/½in dice. Peel the marrow, cut in half and remove the seeds. Chop the flesh into 1cm/½in dice. If you have courgettes instead of marrow, wipe and thinly slice them. Chop the cauliflower into 11cm/4¼in pieces. Chop the onions.

Put all the chopped vegetables into a large bowl and toss in the salt. Leave for 12 hours. Drain the vegetables in a colander, rinse them through with cold water and drain them again.

Pour 600ml/1pt of the vinegar into a non-reactive saucepan and add the mustard seeds, peppercorns and chilli peppers. Bring to the boil and simmer, covered, for 10 minutes. Strain the vinegar and return it to the saucepan.

Put the ginger, turmeric, mustard powder and flour into a small bowl and gradually mix in the unused vinegar. Stir the mixture into the hot vinegar in the saucepan. Bring the mixture to the boil and stir in the vegetables. Simmer for 10 minutes, stirring occasionally.

Allow the pickle to cool completely then pack it into cold, sterilized jars. Seal the jars immediately.

LEFT: Piccalilli

GREEN TOMATO *and* APPLE RELISH

The tomatoes and cooking apple in this hot, bitter-sweet relish provide all the necessary sharpness. The relish can be used on the day that it is made or it can be kept in a covered container in the refrigerator for up to two weeks.

MAKES ABOUT 450ML/¾PT

12 green tomatoes (about 500g • 1lb)
4 green chilli peppers
2 onions (about 250g • 8oz)
1 cooking apple (about 250g • 8lb)
4tbsp olive oil
¼tsp ground allspice
¼tsp salt
2tbsp light muscovado sugar

Put the tomatoes into simmering water and simmer them for 15 minutes. Remove the saucepan from the heat. Skin and finely chop the tomatoes, taking each one out of the saucepan when you are ready to peel it.

Core, seed and finely chop the chilli peppers. Finely chop the onions. Peel, core and chop the apple.

Heat the oil in a saucepan over a low heat. Put in the onion and cook for about 3 minutes until softened. Add the tomatoes, chilli peppers, apple, allspice, salt and sugar. Simmer them, covered, for 20 minutes, to make a thick, pureéd mixture.

Turn the relish into a bowl and allow it to cool then serve.

Red Onion Relish

Based on a Mexican recipe, this mild, crisp and light purple-red relish will add interest to casserole and rice dishes. It may be eaten the day after preparation but will keep for up to one month if bottled. Once opened, it must be stored, covered, in the refrigerator and eaten within one week.

FILLS ABOUT TWO 500G/1LB JARS

4 large red onions (about 500g • 1lb)
1tbsp salt
1tsp dried oregano or marjoram
300ml • ½pt white wine vinegar
½ lemon, juice only

Thinly slice the onions. Put them into a bowl and scatter them with the salt. Leave for 30 minutes.

Pour boiling water over the onions and drain them immediately. Allow them to cool.

When the onions are completely cold, pack them into cold, sterilized jars, adding a little of the oregano or marjoram to each jar.

In a bowl or jug, mix together the white wine vinegar and lemon juice with 6 tablespoons of water and pour over the onion slices. Seal the jars immediately.

SWEETCORN *and* CHILLI RELISH

The sweetcorn kernels used to make this light, unthickened relish should either be freshly cut from the cob or frozen; tinned kernels would not hold their shape to give the relish its textured structure. You can either use the relish immediately or you can bottle it for use within two months; once opened, it should be used within one week.

FILLS ABOUT ONE AND A HALF 500G/1LB JARS

2 green or red chilli peppers
1 green sweet pepper
175g • 6oz sweetcorn kernels
2tbsp caster sugar
½tsp salt
½tsp mustard powder
450ml • ¾pt white wine vinegar

Core and seed the chilli peppers and finely chop them. Core, seed and finely chop the sweet pepper. Put the chilli and sweet peppers into a non-reactive saucepan and add the sweetcorn.

In a bowl, mix together the sugar, salt and mustard powder. Gradually stir in the vinegar then pour the mixture into the saucepan.

Set the pan over a medium heat and bring the contents to the boil. Simmer, uncovered, for 15 minutes, or until the sweetcorn is just tender.

Allow the relish to cool completely and serve immediately or store it in a covered container in the refrigerator for use within one week. Alternatively, spoon it, while still warm, into warm, sterilized jars and seal immediately.

PICKLED BLACKBERRIES

Blackberries make an eye-catching purple pickle with a rich, fruity flavour that is good with all kinds of cold meats. Leave the pickle for one week before using. Unopened, it will keep for up to one year.

FILLS ABOUT THREE 500G/1LB JARS

2tbsp allspice berries
4 cloves
2.5cm • 1in piece cinnamon stick
small piece dried root ginger, bruised
450ml • ¾pt malt vinegar
1.5kg • 3lb blackberries
375g • 12oz Demerara sugar

Put the allspice berries, cloves, cinnamon and ginger into a non-reactive saucepan and pour in the vinegar. Bring gently to the boil, cover and simmer for 10 minutes.

Strain the spiced vinegar into a bowl. Add the blackberries while it is still warm, cover and leave for 12 hours.

Strain the blackberries, reserving the spiced vinegar. Pour the vinegar into a saucepan, add the sugar and bring to the boil. Put in the blackberries and simmer, uncovered, for 10 minutes, or until the blackberries are tender but still retain their shape.

Using a slotted spoon, lift out the blackberries and put them into warm, sterilized jars. Pour the spiced vinegar syrup over them and seal immediately.

RIGHT: Sweetcorn and Chilli Relish

WALNUT *and* CORIANDER RELISH

Based on an Indian recipe from Kashmir, this rich walnut relish is a good accompaniment for curry. It should be eaten as soon after preparation as possible.

MAKES ABOUT 250ML/8FL OZ

125g • 4oz shelled walnuts
6tbsp chopped fresh coriander
½ lemon, juice only
¼tsp cayenne pepper
4tbsp natural yoghurt

Put the walnuts into a food processor and finely chop them. Add all the remaining ingredients and work into a paste.

MUSHROOM RELISH

This rich, delicately flavoured relish can be served immediately it is prepared or stored in the refrigerator in a covered container for up to two weeks. It can also be bottled and kept, unopened, for up to one month.

FILLS ONE 500G/1LB JAR

250g • 8oz open mushrooms
1 onion (about 125g • 4oz)
1 clove garlic
3tbsp olive or sunflower oil
6tbsp red wine vinegar
4tbsp chopped fresh parsley
½tsp black peppercorns, coarsely crushed

Very finely chop the mushrooms, preferably using a food processor. Finely chop the onion and garlic.

Heat the oil in a non-reactive saucepan over a low heat. Put in the onion and garlic and cook for about 3 minutes to soften them.

Raise the heat to medium. Pour in the vinegar and bring it to the boil. Add the mushrooms, parsley and peppercorns. Bring them to the boil, lower the heat and simmer, uncovered, for 10 minutes, or until the mushrooms are cooked through.

Either allow the relish to cool and serve, or spoon it while still hot into a warm, sterilized jar and seal immediately.

RIGHT: Walnut and Coriander Relish

RECIPES

Winter

~

Winter is an ideal time for mixing the mundane with exotic, the savoury with the sweet, to produce pickles and chutneys with rich, warm colours and spicy-hot flavours to cheer up the long, dark days.

~

WINTER

WINTER DAYS MAY BE LONG AND DARK, BUT HAPPILY THE COLOURS OF WINTER FOODS ARE RICH AND WARM. FILL YOUR JARS WITH ORANGE CARROTS AND YELLOW SWEDES, PURPLE-RED CABBAGE AND BEETROOT AND CRIMSON CRANBERRIES.

Make your winter chutneys full flavoured and spicy, with a touch of hotness to warm you through chilly days. Make pickles that are robust enough to contrast well with warming winter casseroles and stews as well as being ideal complements to the roast meats and cold spreads of Christmas.

Ingredients at this time of year are full of contrasts. On the one hand there are roots and cabbages and on the other all the special dried fruits and nuts which are brought to prominence for the period leading up to Christmas. There are plenty of fresh fruits, too, apples and pears which keep well in store, lemons, limes and sweet and Seville oranges, plus big, juicy pineapples, black and white grapes and bananas. Winter is an ideal time for mixing the mundane with the exotic, the acid with the sweet, to produce savoury preserves for your own table and also for giving away as presents.

At one time, before fruit could be stored for long periods or transported across the world, most fresh fruits were used up by mid-winter and all that was left were home dried apples and, if you could afford them, imported dried fruits. That is why most of our traditional Christmas foods have dried fruits as their main ingredient. Think of mince pies, Christmas puddings, and the large rich fruit cake.

Dried fruits are full of concentrated sweetness. For many years, when sugar was relatively more expensive than it is today, dried fruits took its place in a wide variety of recipes. Now, both dried fruits and sugar are readily available and can be used together to enhance the flavours and textures of wintertime preserves. Besides the usual currants, raisins and sultanas, look out for the extra large seedless raisins, plump, whole apricots, moist figs and dates, shiny black prunes, halved pears and whole or halved peaches.

Chopped candied peel can make an interesting bitter-sweet addition to chutneys so it is well worth buying some at the same time as your dried fruits. You can buy it in the piece, in which case it has greater preserving qualities, or, for greater convenience, ready chopped and in a light coating of sugar syrup.

The big advantage in buying dried fruits is that they keep well so, if you find varieties that are available only at this time of the year (peaches or pears for example), buy them now. Put them, still in their packets, into an air-tight container and store them for up to four months in a cool cupboard.

All dried fruits can be added to chutneys to replace some of the sugar content and to add colour and texture. Whole raisins, for example, will make a very dark, rich chutney, somewhat lumpy in texture because some of the fruits stay whole. Whole dried apricots will cook down to a thick, light orange purée (page 113).

BELOW: The best dried fruits can be bought in the winter. Used in chutneys to replace some of the sugar, they will give both flavour and sweetness.

RIGHT: Autumn's apples and pears are still available and in good condition throughout the winter months.

Apples.
1 Kernel Pearmain SDE
2 Green Reinette SDE
3 Yellow Reinette SDE
4 Harvey Pippin SDE
5 Great Gold.n Russell SDE
6 St. Francis SDE
7 Russell Pearmain SDE
8 Golden Pippin SDE
9 Carolina SDE
10 White Ice SDE
11 Loans Pearmain SDE
Pears.
12 Best Chaumontel DES
13 Sheppard's Golden Bell DES
14 Winter Catherine DEE
15 Royal D'Hyver DEW
JANUARY 1732
16 Winter Lemon SDE
17 Golden Boon DEE
18 St. Germain from a Dwarf SDE
19 Lapen D'Hyver DES
20 Winterthorn DEE
21 Lemmintons Chaumontel DES
22 Louise Boon DES
23 Muscat Almaine DEE
24 Petit Boon DES
A Burnett leav'd Rose
B The Yellow Berried Holly S
C Winter Crack SD
D Italian Privett S
E Cockspurthorn S
F Yellow Azarole SD
Design'd by P.tr Casteels.
From the Collection of Robt. Furber Gardiner at Kensington 1732.
Engrav'd by G. Vander Gucht.

Above: Fresh oranges brighten up winter days. Pickle them whole or in slices or use their juice and zest for flavour.

The smaller dried fruits are added whole to chutneys and the larger ones are usually chopped finely or minced before the ingredients are mixed. To make them cook down more quickly, all dried fruits can be soaked for a time before the chutney is made. The best way of keeping their flavour for the chutney and not throwing it out with the soaking water is to soak the fruits in the vinegar that you are going to use in the final making.

Dried Fruits

In the Middle East, dried fruits are made into pickles in which they constitute the single main ingredient. They are soaked in vinegar and then cooked with spices and flavourings to a purée, making the end result really more like a chutney than a pickle in texture. In more Western-style pickles, where crispy, uncooked main ingredients are steeped in spiced vinegar, whole raisins, currants or sultanas can be added to the jars to the advantage of flavour, texture and appearance.

Citrus fruits are all in peak condition during the winter. The juices and grated rinds of oranges, lemons and limes can all be added to chutneys and relishes and thinly pared strips of peel can give colour and flavour to winter pickles. Oranges were not historically used as a pickling fruit. In the Western world, they were treated with suspicion until the seventeenth century and later were more often candied and made into sweet preserves, their savoury potential going unrecognized. Sliced sweet oranges, however, make a delicious bitter-sweet pickle which is excellent with poultry and game (page 120). Seville oranges, the bitter type that are often used for marmalade, have a short winter season, usually around December and January. In most recipes that specify lemon juice, you can use Seville orange juice instead to give your pickle or chutney a light, bitter-orange flavour.

Small, soft citrus fruit, such as clementines and satsumas, can actually be pickled whole, using the same recipe as for orange slices (page 120). Be careful when choosing fruit for this purpose, that you find varieties with few or no pips.

Whole Fruits

Both lemons and limes can be pickled sliced or whole (page 116). They can also be chopped up very finely and added to chutney mixtures. There are recipes for pickled whole lemons that date from the eighteenth and nineteenth centuries and which have changed very little over the years. The process begins with slitting the lemons into quarters but still

LEFT: Beetroot can be made into jewel coloured pickles and quickly prepared relishes.

joined at one end, and then packing them with salt. There are various methods for covering them with spiced vinegar, brine or oil, processes that you will find in books of Middle Eastern cookery today.

Citrus fruits can be bought well in advance of using and will keep for several weeks in a cool, dry larder, but, as with all fruits, the sooner they are used the better they will taste. The skins of most citrus fruits are waxed and so, if you are pickling them whole or unpeeled, it is best to scrub them before using.

Fresh cranberries are another winter speciality. They ripen in the autumn but soften and mellow in the winter frosts to be ready for converting into relishes for the Thanksgiving turkey. Cranberries keep exceptionally well. They are usually sold vacuum packed and as such will keep in the refrigerator for up to one month. Frozen ones can also be used. Pineapples and bananas are available all the year round in most countries, but, in the northern hemisphere at least, they are at their best in winter.

Pineapples have been regarded as such an exotic fruit, that there are few pickle or chutney recipes for them, at least in Western cookery books (page 125). The attitude has been that a pineapple should be appreciated in its natural state. However, pineapple relishes are popular in South-East Asia, there are Indian recipes for pineapple chutney and John Evelyn, writing in England in the seventeenth century, recommended pineapple as a fruit for pickling, although he did not give a recipe. The pineapple is a refreshing fruit and contrasts well with hot curries and other spicy foods. It will keep for up to a week in a cool, dry larder.

Bananas have a soft, creamy texture and sweet flavour that makes them ideal for chutneys (page 114). Add a little orange, lemon or lime juice and you have a perfect combination. In India and the Middle East, mashed banana with lime or lemon juice, spices and yoghurt makes a quickly prepared relish or sambal to go with warming, spicy foods. Use bananas that are ripe but not over-ripe. The skins should be a good bright yellow but without any brown patches. Store them in a cool, dry larder for up to two days.

Another popular sambal ingredient is coconut and it always tastes better used fresh (page 118). To prepare a coconut, first remove the tufts of coarse hair. Then pierce the "eyes" with a skewer and let the liquid drain into a bowl. Place the coconut on a firm surface and hit it firmly with a hammer all round the centre to make the outer shell split. Remove the shell, cut the inner flesh into pieces and cut away the hard, brown rind. Then grate the flesh, either by hand or using a food processor.

VEGETABLES

Most winter vegetables can be turned into some sort of savoury preserve. Crunchy celery and Florence fennel were both popular pickle ingredients in the eighteenth and nineteenth centuries. They make light flavoured, crisp pickles and relishes (page 122). Both red and white cabbage can be pickled and, in Germany, white cabbage is made into a fermented pickle called sauerkraut which can take up to a month to prepare and which is served with salted meats and sausages.

Of the root vegetables, carrots, beetroot and turnips are the most used and swedes can be put into chutneys. Carrots can be pickled raw, either sliced or in thin sticks. In some older recipes, where they are the single ingredient, they are boiled until they are tender before being put into the pickling vinegar. Beetroot pickle has always been a popular inclusion on the cold table. In the eighteenth and nineteenth centuries it was valued as much for its colour as for its flavour and it was used as a garnish for salads and cold meals. Turnip pickles and relishes are not so popular in the West but are quite common in the Middle East and well worth trying.

In the nineteenth century, many American country homes had a root cellar, where home-grown root vegetables would be stored from autumn to the end of winter. Now, however, our houses are too warm. Root vegetables are best bought when you need them and stored in a cool place for up to one week. The best way we have, in fact, of storing vegetables, is to make them into winter preserves.

APPLE *and* DATE CHUTNEY

Dark and thick, this farmhouse-style chutney is hot, spicy and sweet. For bitter-sweet chutney, you may replace 125g/4oz of the dates with chopped candied peel. Leave the chutney for at least two weeks before opening. Unopened, it will keep for up to two years.

FILLS FIVE TO SIX 500G/1LB JARS

1kg • 2lb stoned dried dates
4 onions (about 500g • 1lb)
4 large cooking apples (about 1kg • 2lb)
125g • 4oz dark muscovado sugar
180g • 6oz black treacle
600ml • 1pt cider vinegar
1tsp salt
1tsp cayenne pepper
1tsp ground allspice

Finely chop or mince the dates and onions. Peel, core and finely chop or mince the apples.

Put the chopped dates, onions and apples into a preserving pan or non-reactive saucepan and add all the remaining ingredients. Bring slowly to the boil, turn down the heat and simmer, uncovered and stirring occasionally, for 1¼ hours, or until the mixture forms a thick, dark chutney.

Spoon the hot chutney into warm, sterilized jars and seal immediately.

APRICOT, CARROT *and* SWEDE CHUTNEY

The pieces of swede and carrot remain slightly crunchy giving this hot, light-flavoured amber chutney an interesting texture. It is ready to eat after two weeks. Unopened, it will keep for up to one year.

FILLS ABOUT FOUR 500G/1LB JARS

500g • 1lb dried whole apricots
900ml • 1½pt distilled malt vinegar
5 large carrots (about 500g • 1lb)
1 small swede (about 500g • 1lb)
4 onions (about 500g • 1lb)
250g • 8oz Demerara sugar
2tsp ground mace
2tsp cayenne pepper

Soak the apricots, whole, for 12 hours in half of the vinegar. Drain and chop them, reserving the vinegar.

Peel and finely chop the carrots, swede and onions.

Put the chopped apricots, carrots, swede and onions into a preserving pan or non-reactive saucepan with the sugar, mace and cayenne pepper. Pour in the reserved and the unused vinegar and bring slowly to the boil. Turn the heat down and simmer gently, uncovered and stirring occasionally, for 1 hour, or until the mixture is soft and thick.

Spoon the hot chutney into warm, sterilized jars and seal immediately.

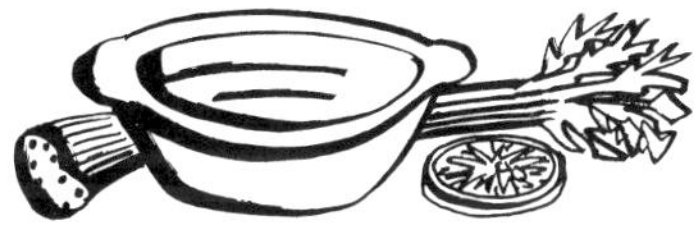

PICKLED BEETROOT *with* HORSERADISH

The deep red of this unusual, spicy beetroot pickle is flecked with the lighter colour of pieces of horseradish. Few people have access to fresh horseradish root but preserved ready-grated horseradish is widely available in conveniently small jars. If you are lucky enough to obtain fresh horseradish, scrub it well and chop it finely in a food processor rather than grate it by hand, which is a slow process releasing unpleasantly pungent fumes. Leave the pickle for one week before using. Unopened, it will keep for up to six months but once opened, it should be eaten within one week.

FILLS ABOUT FIVE 500G/1LB JARS

900ml • 1½pt white wine vinegar
2tsp allspice berries
2tsp black peppercorns
2 pieces blade mace
2tbsp juniper berries
12 whole beetroot (about 1.5kg • 3lb), uncooked and scrubbed
180g • 6oz horseradish, fresh or preserved, grated

Pour the vinegar into a non-reactive saucepan and add the allspice berries, black peppercorns, mace and 2 teaspoons of the juniper berries. Bring slowly to the boil over a low heat. Remove the saucepan from the heat, cover and leave for 2 hours then strain.

Boil the beetroot whole, in their skins, for 45 minutes, or until they are tender. Drain then peel and dice them while they are still warm.

Crush the remaining juniper berries, either by using a pestle and mortar or with the handle of a heavy knife.

In a bowl, mix together the beetroot, horseradish and juniper berries then pack the mixture into cold, sterilized jars. Pour in the cold spiced vinegar to cover and seal immediately.

PICKLED RED CABBAGE *and* CARROTS

Floating strands of carrot add orange highlights to the overall crimson-purple of this crunchy, savoury pickle. Leave it for four days before using. Once opened, it should be eaten within one week but unopened it will keep for two months.

FILLS ABOUT SIX 500G/1LB JARS

1 red cabbage
2-3 carrots (about 250g • 8oz)
3tbsp salt
900ml • 1½pt malt vinegar
1tsp cloves
1tsp mustard seeds
1tsp allspice berries
1tsp black peppercorns
4 pieces blade mace

Finely shred the cabbage and cut the carrots into julienne sticks. Layer the cabbage and carrots in a bowl with the salt. Cover and leave for 12 hours, shaking the bowl occasionally.

Pour the vinegar into a non-reactive saucepan and add the cloves, mustard seeds, allspice berries, peppercorns and mace. Set the saucepan over a low heat and slowly bring the contents to the boil. Remove the saucepan from the heat, cover the vinegar, and leave to cool completely.

Drain the cabbage and carrots in a colander and pack them into cold, sterilized jars. Strain the cold vinegar and pour it into the jars to cover the vegetables. Seal immediately.

BANANA *and* RAISIN CHUTNEY

The flavour of this light brown chutney dotted with dark raisins is sweet, dry and spicy. Ready to eat after two weeks, unopened, it will keep for up to one year.

FILLS ABOUT FIVE 500G/1LB JARS

12 bananas
6 onions (about 750g • 1½lb)
2 cloves garlic
1tsp salt
1 large orange, grated rind and juice
500g • 1lb raisins
1½tbsp ground cumin
1½tbsp ground cardamom
2tsp ground coriander
1tsp cayenne pepper
600ml • 1pt white wine vinegar

Peel and finely chop or mince the bananas and the onions. Crush the garlic with the salt.

Put the chopped bananas and onions with the crushed garlic into a preserving pan or non-reactive saucepan. Add all the remaining ingredients and mix together. Set the saucepan over a low heat, bring slowly to the boil and simmer for 1¼ hours, or until the mixture is thick.

Spoon the hot chutney into warm, sterilized jars and seal immediately.

RIGHT: Pickled Red Cabbage and Carrots

FIG CHUTNEY

Dried figs are extremely sugary and make a dark, rich and sweet chutney. Leave it for at least two weeks before using. Unopened, it will keep for up to two years.

FILLS ABOUT TWO 500G/1LB JARS

900ml • 1½pt white wine vinegar
2tsp black peppercorns
1tbsp allspice berries
1tbsp cloves
1kg • 2lb whole dried figs
500g • 1lb Demerara sugar
1tsp cayenne pepper
2tsp ground cinnamon
2tsp ground mace

Pour half of the white wine vinegar into a non-reactive saucepan and add the peppercorns, allspice berries and cloves. Bring to the boil and simmer, covered, for 5 minutes.

Strain the vinegar into a large bowl. Put in the figs and leave them for 2 hours. Drain the figs, reserving the vinegar, and finely chop them, removing the small piece of stalk from each one.

Pour the reserved vinegar together with the unused vinegar into a preserving pan or non-reactive saucepan and add the chopped figs, sugar, cayenne pepper, cinnamon and mace. Bring gently to the boil and simmer for 1¼ hours, or until the mixture is reduced to a thick paste. Stir frequently as the figs make a very thick purée.

Spoon the hot chutney into warm, sterilized jars and seal immediately.

LEMONS *and* LIMES *pickled in* OIL

The unlikely combination of ingredients produces a bitter pickle that is surprisingly good with rich, spiced dishes. As the lemons and limes are used whole, buy unwaxed fruit if possible; if you cannot find any, scrub well before using. Leave the pickle for three weeks before using. Unopened, it will keep for up to three months. Once opened it should be eaten within a week.

FILLS ABOUT FOUR 500G/1LB JARS

6 lemons
6 limes
4tbsp salt
2tsp allspice berries
2tsp coriander seeds
4 bay leaves
8 dried chilli peppers
7501ml • 1¼pt sunflower oil

Scrub the lemons and limes and slice them thinly. Put them into a colander and sprinkle them with the salt. Leave for 24 hours then drain them.

Pack the citrus slices into cold, sterilized jars, sprinkling a few allspice berries and coriander seeds in each jar. Push one bay leaf and two dried chilli peppers into each jar. Fill the jars with the oil and seal immediately.

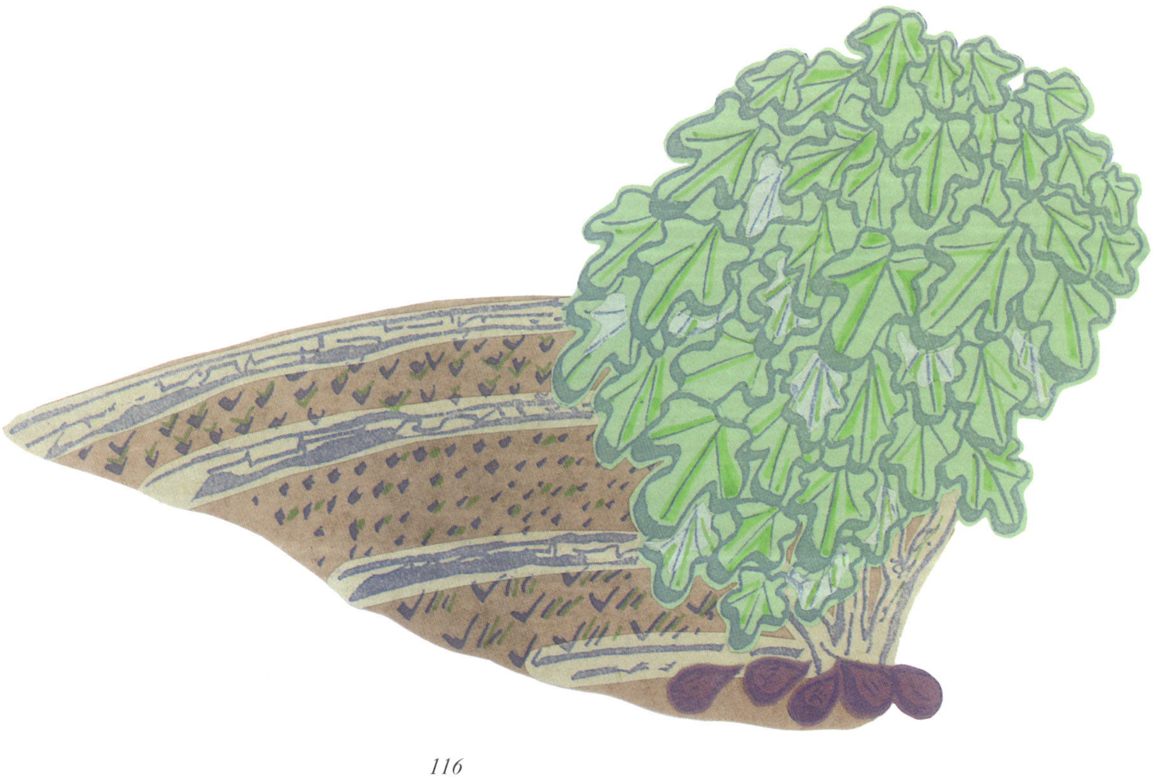

YOGHURT *and* COCONUT RELISH

Creamy, refreshing and extraordinarily simple to make, this is the perfect relish to accompany a curry and counteract its hotness. Buy an unwaxed lime if you can; if not, scrub the fruit well. The relish will keep for up to 24 hours in a covered container in the refrigerator.

MAKES ABOUT 300ML/½PT

125g • 4oz freshly grated coconut
1 small onion, very finely chopped (optional)
1 lime, grated rind and juice
½tsp cayenne pepper
½tsp ground cumin
4tbsp natural yoghurt

Mix all the ingredients together and leave them to stand for at least 2 hours before serving.

SWEET ONION *and* LIME RELISH

No vinegar is used to make this relish composed of softened and browned onions coated in a sweet and sour sauce. Instead, all the necessary acidity is supplied by the limes. Buy unwaxed limes; if you cannot find any, scrub the fruit well. The relish will keep for up to one month if stored in a covered container in the refrigerator. Bottled, it will keep for up to two months.

FILLS ONE 500G/1LB JAR

3 large onions (about 375g • 12oz)
2 limes, grated rind and juice only
2tbsp dark muscovado sugar
½tsp cayenne pepper
2tbsp sunflower oil

Cut the onions in half lengthways and thinly slice each in half crossways.

Put the sliced onions together with all the remaining ingredients into a saucepan. Cover, set over a high heat and bring gently to the boil. Turn the heat to the lowest point so the onions are just simmering and cook gently for about 1 hour, stirring occasionally, until the onions are soft and brown and the mixture is dry but not too sticky.

Allow to cool and serve. Alternatively, spoon the hot relish into a warm, sterilized jar and seal immediately.

ORANGES *in* HONEYED VINEGAR

Bitter-sweet orange slices steeped in a mild honey vinegar are excellent with game and poultry. Leave the pickle for one week before using. Unopened, it will keep for up to six months. Once opened, it should be eaten within one week.

FILLS ABOUT FOUR 500G/1LB JARS

10 sweet, juicy oranges, seedless if possible
600ml • 1pt white wine vinegar
300g • 10oz clear honey
1 cinnamon stick
1 small piece dried ginger root, bruised
2tsp cloves

Scrub and thinly slice the oranges, removing any pips. Put the orange slices into a non-reactive saucepan and pour in enough water to just cover them. Set them over a low heat, bring slowly to the boil and simmer gently for about 40 minutes, or until the peel is soft but the flesh is still intact. Lift out the oranges using a perforated spoon. Reserve 300ml/½pt of the liquid.

Pour the vinegar and the reserved liquid into a non-reactive saucepan, add the honey, cinnamon stick, ginger root and cloves and bring to the boil. Add the orange slices and simmer gently, uncovered, for 15 minutes, or until the rind becomes slightly translucent.

Using the perforated spoon, transfer the orange slices to warm jars. Boil the vinegar liquid for a further 5 minutes. Remove the cinnamon stick and ginger root and pour the hot, spiced liquid over the oranges, allowing an even number of cloves to fall into each jar. Seal immediately.

Raw Cranberry Relish

The uncooked fruits give this deep crimson relish a refreshing bitter-sweet taste. It is a seasonal accompaniment to roast meats and game. Defrosted frozen cranberries can be used if fresh ones are unavailable. The relish will keep for up to one week in a covered jar in the refrigerator if you do not add the chopped orange until just before serving.

MAKES ABOUT 450ML/¾PINT

2 large oranges
250g • 8oz cranberries, fresh or frozen and thawed
2tbsp red wine vinegar
2tbsp sunflower oil
1 onion (about 125g • 4oz)
½tsp ground allspice
50g • 2oz sugar

Squeeze the juice from one of the oranges and cut off the rind. Pour the juice with the rind into a food processor, add the cranberries and red wine vinegar and work them to a rough purée.

Heat the oil in a frying pan over a low heat. Add the onion and allspice and cook for about 3 minutes until the onion is soft. Add the sugar and stir until it melts.

Add the onion and sugar mixture to the cranberries in the food processor and process again to a purée. Turn the mixture into a bowl.

Cut the rind and pith from the remaining orange and finely chop the flesh. Mix the orange flesh into the cranberry mixture.

Serve the relish chilled, on the day that it is prepared.

Chrane *with* Raisins

Chrane is a Jewish relish made of beetroot and horseradish that is usually served with salt beef. In this version, the addition of raisins introduces a sweeter quality. If you are using fresh horseradish, scrub it well and finely chop in a food processor rather than grate it by hand, a slow process which releases unpleasantly pungent fumes. The relish can be eaten on the day that it is made, but it will last for up to a week in a covered container in the refrigerator. In a sealed, sterilized jar, it will keep for up to three months.

FILLS ONE 500G/1LB JAR

2 beetroot (about 250g • 4oz), uncooked and with skin
6tbsp horseradish, fresh or preserved, grated
3tbsp raisins
6tbsp red wine vinegar

Boil the beetroot whole, in their skins for 45 minutes, or until they are tender. Drain and peel them then finely grate them.

Mix the grated beetroot with the grated horseradish, raisins and red wine vinegar.

Place the relish into a covered container and leave for at least 4 hours before serving. Alternatively, spoon it hot into a warm, sterilized jar and seal immediately.

Chinese Pickles

Made with brine instead of vinegar, this interesting mixed vegetable pickle is crisp and light. Leave it for four days before using. Unopened, it will keep for up to one month. Once opened, it should be eaten as soon as possible.

FILLS ABOUT TEN 500G/1LB JARS

½ small white cabbage (about 500g • 1lb)
4 white turnips (about 500g • 1lb)
1 head celery
1 cucumber
6 dried chilli peppers
6 thin slices fresh ginger root
1tsp black peppercorns
125g • 4oz salt
4tbsp Chinese rice wine or dry sherry

Finely shred the cabbage. Scrub the turnips, peel them if necessary, and cut them into small, thin sticks. Cut the celery into 2.5cm/1in sticks. Cut the cucumber into quarters lengthways and then into 2.5cm/1in lengths.

Spread the prepared vegetables on clean, dry tea cloths on a tray, cover them with more tea cloths and leave for 3 hours to dry.

Put all the remaining ingredients into a non-reactive saucepan together with 1.75 litres/3pts water and bring to the boil. Turn the heat down and simmer for 5 minutes then remove from the heat. Allow to cool completely then strain, reserving the liquid.

Pack the vegetables into cold, sterilized jars. Pour the cold liquid over them to cover and seal immediately.

CELERY *and* FENNEL RELISH

Rather like a hot salad, this vegetable relish can be served hot as well as cold. Eat it on the day of making or store it in the refrigerator in a covered container for up to three days.

MAKES ABOUT 300ML/½PT

4 large sticks celery
1 small head fennel
1 small onion
1 clove garlic
4tbsp olive oil
½ orange, juice only
2tbsp white wine vinegar
2tsp Dijon mustard

Finely chop the celery, fennel, onion and garlic.

Heat the oil in a frying pan over a medium heat. Put in the finely chopped celery, fennel, onion and garlic and cook them for about 2 minutes, stirring, until the onion begins to look transparent.

Stir in the orange juice, wine vinegar and mustard and bring to the boil.

Remove the pan from the heat. Transfer the relish to a small dish and serve hot or cold.

1LB
8oz

Pineapple *and* Ginger Chutney

More syrupy than most chutneys, this hot and sour version is nonetheless thick enough to hold the pineapple chunks prettily in suspension. Ready to eat after two weeks, unopened, it will keep for up to six months.

FILLS ABOUT FOUR TO FIVE 500G/1LB JARS

2 large pineapples
2tbsp salt
125g • 4oz fresh ginger root
10 cloves garlic
250g • 8oz light soft brown sugar
1tsp ground cinnamon
1tsp ground nutmeg
600ml • 1pt white wine vinegar
375g • 12oz sultanas

Remove the rind from the pineapples. Slice and then finely chop the flesh, removing the cores. Put the pineapple pieces into a bowl, sprinkle them with the salt and leave for 1 hour then drain them.

Peel and grate the ginger root. Peel and crush the garlic cloves. Alternatively, peel and roughly chop the ginger root, put it into a food processor with the garlic cloves and process until they are very finely chopped.

Put the sugar, cinnamon and nutmeg into a preserving pan or non-reactive saucepan, pour in the white wine vinegar and bring to the boil. Add the pineapple, ginger and garlic with the sultanas and simmer gently for 2 hours, or until the liquid has reduced and thickened to a syrupy consistency; it will be more runny than the usual thick, puréed type of chutney but will thicken as it cools.

Spoon the chutney into warm, sterilized jars and seal immediately.

Index

Acknowledgements

Key – (a) above (b) below

Murray Alcosser/Image Bank 6–7, Bodleian Library 8 (a), Nick Nicholson/Image Bank 8 (b), e.t. archive 9, Gabe Palmer/Ace 12–13, Paul Thompson/Ace 14, Hulton Deutsch 15, Mansell Collection 16, e.t. archive 17, Vibert-Stokes/Ace 18, Robert Opie 19, Pictor 20–1, e.t. archive 22, Robert Opie 23 (a), Michael Freeman 23 (b), Michael Freeman 24, Vibert-Stokes/Ace 26–7, Pictor 28, Charles Mahaux/Image Bank 29, Robert Opie 30, Mansell Collection 39, Michael Freeman 42–43, Bodleian Library 44, e.t. archive 45, Mauritius/Ace 46, Tangent/Ace 47, Mauritius/Ace 62–63, Bullaty/Lomeo/Image Bank 64, e.t. archive 65, Bodleian Library 66, e.t. archive 67, J. Allan Cash 82, Anand Razdan/Ace 84–5, David W. Hamilton/Image Bank 86, e.t. archive 87, Trevor Wood/Ace 88, Carol Kohen/Image Bank 89, Michael Freeman 106–7, Lesley Howling/Ace 108, e.t. archive 109, Pictor 110, Bodleian Library 111

We would also like to thank Elizabeth David Cookshop, The Piazza, Covent Garden, London WC2E 8RA for supplying equipment used in photography.